MW01700894

Scott,
Thanks for all your help. Great job!
Leon Kaiser

Scott
Thanks so much for all of your help - you have really been a joy to have in our ... La

Thanks so much: parrigo@bracub.com

Thank You for all your help and I hope you enjoyed all of our Southern Hospitality
Have a safe + Blessed trip Home
Fatima

Scott -
Merci Beaucoup!
Kelly Constantin

Scott,
Hope you had a chance to see our sunset on the river! If not, come back!
Kim

Thanks Scott.
Kate Crigler

Scott,
Thanks for helping make our job that much easier.
Marie

Scott -
It was a pleasure being your "ride" this week - AND I learned something! Next time you visit try to see more of the neat things in the book!
Nancy

Scott -
It's been fun.
Enjoyed the training!
You kept it interesting.
Enjoyed our lunches.
Come again
Julie

Scott
you have to come back to BR + visit the sites + of course eat @ Mike's
GB
P.S. maybe you'll get to meet my boys.

Scott -
Great job on the training! I am so glad you were part of our Amanda's World here in Baton Rouge. Many thanks!
Amanda

Scott,
You're a great trainer + your personality was wonderful. Thanks for all your help
P.S. Strawberries next time you're in Baton Rouge
Stephanie

Scott,
You're a great instructor! Thanks for all your help!
Quilita

In cooperation with

The Chamber of GREATER BATON ROUGE

Baton Rouge

Painting the Town Red
A Celebration of 300 Years

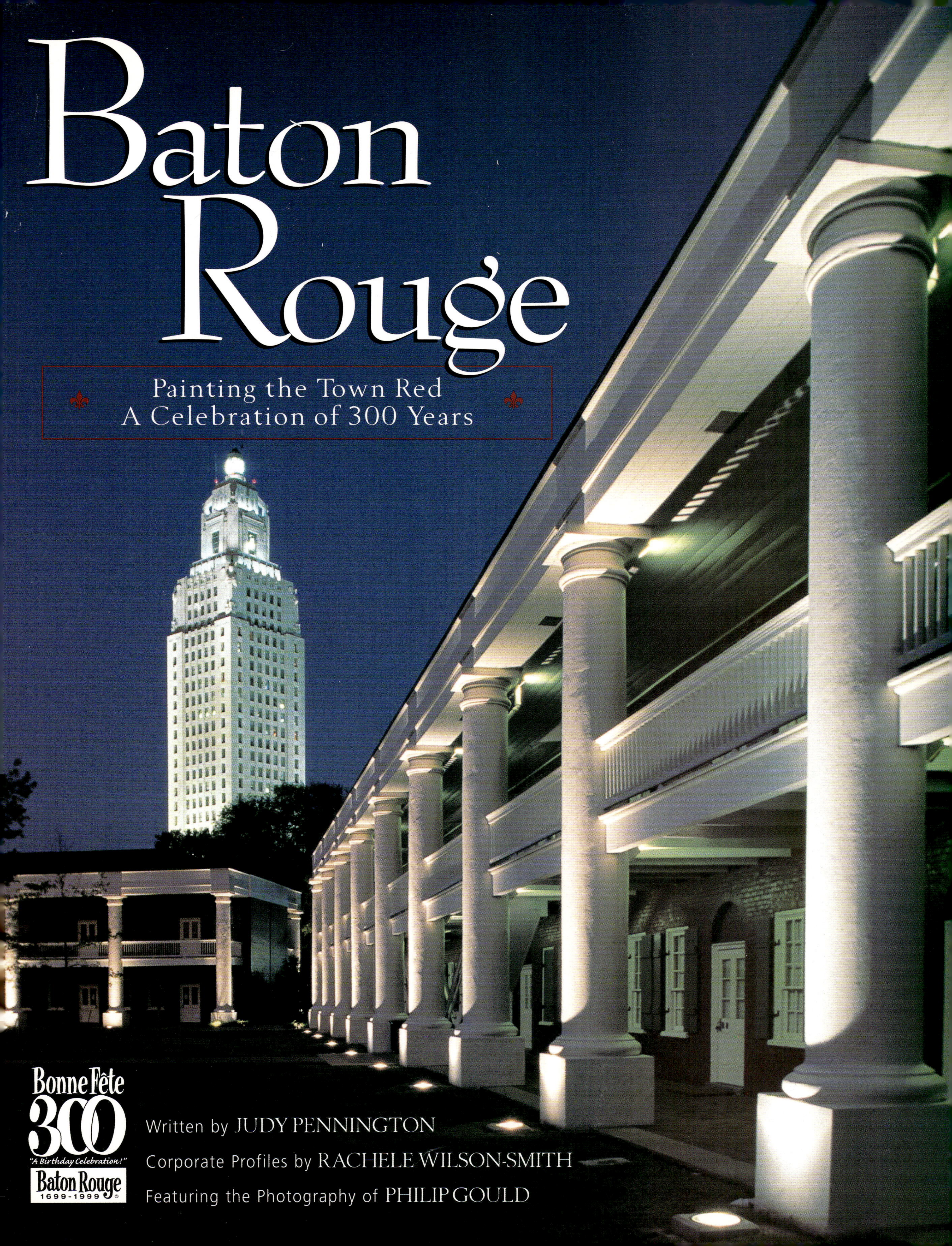

Bonne Fête 300
"A Birthday Celebration!"
Baton Rouge
1699-1999

Written by JUDY PENNINGTON
Corporate Profiles by RACHELE WILSON-SMITH
Featuring the Photography of PHILIP GOULD

Baton Rouge

Painting the Town Red; A Celebration of 300 Years

Produced in cooperation with the
Chamber of Greater Baton Rouge

By Judy Pennington
Corporate profiles by Rachelle Wilson Smith
Featuring the photography of Philip Gould

Staff for Baton Rouge: *Painting the Town Red; A Celebration of 300 Years*

Sales Associates	**Dahlia Davis, Arlaine Niclas**
Acquisitions	**Henry S. Beers**
Executive Editor	**James E. Turner**
Managing Editor	**Wendi Lewis**
Profile Editors	**Kari Jarnot and Mary Catherine Richardson**
Design Director	**Scott Phillips**
Designer	**Eddie Lavoie**
Photo Editors	**Eddie Lavoie and Wendi Lewis**
Production Manager	**Jarrod Stiff**
Editorial Assistants	**Anne Shinn and Amanda Joy Burbank**
Contract Manager	**Christi Stevens**
National Sales Manager	**John Hecker**
Sales Coordinator	**Annette B. Lozier**
Proofreader	**Angela Mann and Amanda Joy Burbank**
Accounting Services	**Sara Ann Turner**
Printing Production	**Gary G. Pulliam**
Pre-press separations	**Artcraft Graphic Productions**

CCI

Community Communications, Inc.
Montgomery, Alabama

James E. Turner, Chairman of the Board
Ronald P. Beers, President
Daniel S. Chambliss, Vice President

Published 1999

First Edition
ISBN Number: 1-885352-61-1
Library of Congress Catalog Number: 99-43645

Contents

Contents

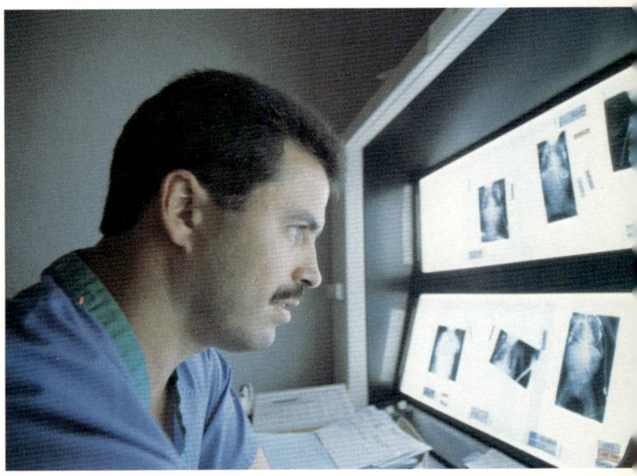

Foreword

Baton Rouge, Louisiana, is a wonderfully unique and dynamic city, where the flavor and charm of the Old South coexists with cutting-edge technology in a thriving industrial and agricultural economy. The Chamber of Greater Baton Rouge is proud to present the story of Louisiana's capital city through this exceptional book.

Baton Rouge is a community where life provides pleasure, opportunity, and growth to its residents in lifestyle and in business—a community that seeks new opportunities through innovative thinking and new relationships. This is a city where some of the world's most advanced industrial facilities share space with antebellum mansions and Native American burial grounds. Cutting-edge technology has chiseled a firm foothold in this thriving industrial and agricultural center that still retains the charm and romance of the Old South. Proud of its history and excited about its future, Baton Rouge provides a peaceful, quiet lifestyle, or all the bustling, metropolitan activity you could ask for—all in one of the most extraordinary places to live and work anywhere in the country.

From the fascinating people that call Baton Rouge home, to the variety of businesses that make up its strong economic base, "Red Stick" has always been a diverse, progressive community. We invite you to experience the excitement that our city has to offer, and to enjoy this detailed look at our history, amenities, and unique culture in the pages that follow.

The Chamber of Greater Baton Rouge plays a major role in our community in the areas of economic and community development, and maintains a strong commitment to making Baton Rouge a regional center of business and culture. If you would like more information on the area, or if Baton Rouge is a destination location for you or your business, contact us. We'll be happy to help.

Jimmy Lyles, CCE
President and CEO
The Chamber of Greater Baton Rouge

Preface

City of kindness. City of hope. City of opportunity.

It's fair to say that Baton Rouge offers these things and that's quite a lot, really—to everyone. But don't take it from me. Read on. In these pages I've written all the good things I knew about my home town and a lot more, especially historical, that I didn't, and which came from in-depth research.

This book has made me consider what I like best about Baton Rouge—like the lively music, art, and cultural festivals downtown, where you walk in the shade of sprawling oak trees and see lots of wonderful people you know, and, year after year, more you want to know.

There's a lot to love here—the heady smell of sweet olive trees abloom in spring, the sparkling red and green lights of the State Capitol at Christmas, the Synchronized Lawn Mover Brigade in the Spanish Town Mardi Gras Parade (a spoof on Louisiana politics). Where else in the world could you feast on such delicious, spicy seafood, dance to Cajun and zydeco bands, and go fishing in a busy, modern state capital with a small town atmosphere? Surely, nowhere else but in Baton Rouge is tailgating a good verb and Mardi Gras a state holiday.

The best thing about Baton Rouge is Baton Rougeans. They are quick to smile at each other and strike up conversations with strangers in grocery store lines. Our cultural diversity and ample elbow room make it easy to find a place of belonging. Here, you can discover the secrets of life in an open, friendly city that is a good place to live, raise children, and gracefully grow old.

Researching this book has deepened my appreciation of the willingness, even eagerness, of community volunteers and activists working to create a better life for everyone. Their inclusiveness is a hopeful sign for the future, as they are listening to the voices of people who are not always heard and answering with real solutions.

Thus my portrait of Baton Rouge, in tribute to their courage and optimism, is a walk on the bright side. It celebrates our city's fascinating history and heritage, its wild green beauty, shimmering waters, sunny horizons, and, more than these things, the generous hearts of so many people reaching out to others.

Bonne Fete, Baton Rouge, and happy birthday, Louisiana. May your three hundred sparkling candles light up the new millennium.

Judy Pennington, author

Part One

At sunset, a river of riches steams golden past the terraced bluffs of Baton Rouge, washing prosperity into the lives of more than half a million people.

Children skip along the levee plaza, laughing in delight as a tiny pushboat steers a long line of cargo barges toward the Gulf of Mexico. Birds dip and wheel above the city dock's graceful arches, a fitting symbol of a modern river capital open to the world.

As the sky reddens, people standing on the dock talk quietly, hushed by the sparkling beauty of commerce on the world's third longest river. Foreign ships glide silently by and they listen to waves splashing on the shore, their sense of peace and place cresting in rhythmic flow.

Night falls. Families and couples walk the levee, nodding to passersby. Behind them, a cascading fountain hisses to remind us that water is the essential element to life. Overhead, a sultry breeze snaps the multicolored flags of seven nations that fought to own this ancient trade route and its fertile, lush green frontiers.

Still untamed, the mighty Mississippi is history itself, bending along the land to shape, cleanse, and enrich it. The water murmurs and sings, whispers and sighs of days gone by: the Father of Waters, the father of tomorrow.

Chapter 1

By the Riverside

Frontier battles over trade. Steamboats, King Cotton, and the Civil War. The political capers of Huey P. Long. For three hundred years, the Red Stick has stirred the currents of history and spiced up America's melting pot.

Rich and poor, young and old, Baton Rougeans know how to celebrate life and the river that is their lifeblood. In the years of their 300th birthday, "Bonne Fete" in French, the people of the capital city have more to celebrate than ever before. Their "gumbo" of cultures, each retaining its distinct flavor, blends tenacity with optimism and ingenuity with a *joie de vivre* that makes Baton Rouge unique throughout the world.

For most people, thoughts of the Mississippi River tend to conjure up the lyrics to the Broadway tune, "Ol' Man River:" "He don't say nothin'/He just keeps rollin'." But in this city, a center of trade for thousands of years, the song of the river is work. Down by the riverside, as the gospel hymn says, people work even harder than they play and, to do so, must "lay aside their swords and shields" and "join hands with everyone."

Most of the capital city's first three hundred years blazed with struggle, conflict, and intrigue. Today, one of the buildings of the U.S. Arsenal, constructed in 1835 as part of the Pentagon Barracks, may be seen on the grounds of the new State Capitol. *Photo by Philip Gould*

It has not always been so, and, in fact, most of the capital city's first three hundred years blazed with struggle, conflict, and intrigue.

Baton Rouge's story begins some eight thousand years ago, when hunters chased mastodons into lush woodlands across bayous and rivers and settled here to enjoy the abundant food and waterway trade routes. By at least 4000 B.C. they were living on the "high land" ridge (today Highland, Old Perkins, and Bluff roads) nearly encircling the present-day Spanish Lake Basin.

By 2000 B.C., native people paddled their cypress canoes upriver to trade at Poverty Point, a bustling metropolis and ceremonial center that exchanged goods with tribes all the way from northeast Louisiana, near Monroe, to the great Lakes. From 500 B.C. until 1500 A.D., the tribe fished, hunted, planted crops, and lived in a large village on the north bank of Bayou Manchac at Alligator Bayou (the lowlands edge of the present-day Country Club of Louisiana). The village was then, as Baton Rouge is today, the regional seat of political power.

A Spanish explorer, Hernando de Soto, paddled past the future site of Baton Rouge in 1542, but a Frenchman would claim the vast river valley known as Louisiana. In April 1682, Rene Robert Cavelier, Sieur de LaSalle floated an expedition downriver to the mouth of the

From its earliest days, Baton Rouge has drawn strength from its position on the Mississippi River. *Photo by Philip Gould*

Mississippi, unfurled the flag of Bourbon, France, and claimed the valley for his sovereign, Louis XIV. The French king sent LaSalle to hunt for gold in Mexico, but LaSalle was enchanted with Louisiana and did not forget her. Later, he convinced his government to let

During its three hundred years, Baton Rouge has operated under the flags of France, Britain, Spain, the Republic of West Florida, the secessionist flag of Louisiana, the flag of the Confederacy, and the flag of the United States of America. *Photo by Philip Gould*

him plant a colony at the mouth of the Mississippi, so that France could gain control of the river trade route and colonization in the heartland of Europe's "new" world.

Unfortunately, LaSalle could not again find the mouth of the river again. After two years of searching, he was murdered by his tired, aggrieved men.

Fifteen years later, with Spanish and British royals eyeing the river and its fertile valleys, France sent a party of French-Canadian naval officers to stake a colony. Paddling upriver, Pierre Le Moyne, Sieur d'Iberville was welcomed by native people living in a Bayougoula village. A few days later, he left the village, paddled upriver a few leagues, and, on March 17, 1699, sighted a red stick or, in French, baton rouge, on high bluffs towering over the river. The stick or pole, dripping with bloody fish and animal heads, is believed to have been the hunting boundary of the Houma and Bayougoula Indians but could have been simply a skinning post. Regardless, Iberville admired the beauty of this virgin paradise. Buffalo and deer roamed the high meadows of the bluffs, and alligators, turtles, ducks, and beaver lived in the wetlands below.

Eight days later, on March 25, 1699, a Bayougoula guide led Iberville and his party five leagues downriver to a stream winding inward from the Mississippi's east bank. The explorers spent the night on a pirogue landing at Alligator Bayou, again noted the beauty of the place, and paddled along Bayou Manchac, the Amite River, Lakes Maurepas, and Lake Pontchartrain all the way to the Gulf of Mexico.

Iberville had found a site for his colony, which could be supplied more easily by this route than by the twisting Mississippi River. Bayou Manchac, Choctaw words for "slow-moving stream" and "back door" entrance to the Gulf, saved ten days of upriver struggle against the swift, dangerous currents of the Mississippi.

In 1718, Baton Rouge's first citizen, Bernard Diron Dartaguette, farmed a land grant at the confluence of Bayou Manchac and the Mississippi River but vanished without a trace a few years later. Primarily French and German families settled on rich lands along the river until the end of the French and Indian War in 1763.

In the settlement treatment, the wily French claimed that the lakes and bayous between Bayou Manchac and the Gulf Coast formed an

Prosperity was ushered in by the 1812 arrival of the steamboat New Orleans. Baton Rouge's edge on trade was visible on the riverfront, where mercantile stores, warehouses, inns, and taverns crowded together in a row.
Historic image courtesy of the Catholic Diocese of Baton Rouge

island. Since islands were not subject to forfeiture, the British, who had poor maps and seemed not to recognize the importance of the New Orleans port, allowed the French to keep the territory. The French government ceded it to Spain in compensation for war losses, thus making Bayou Manchac an international boundary line between the Spanish and the British in the New World. Suddenly, these longtime imperial foes were a "bowshot" apart from each other on the shady little bayou.

Both nations hastily dealt out land grants to settlers who would defend their territories. The British built Fort Bute just north of the bayou and granted lands along the river and the basin's "high land" ridge to English, Scottish, and Irish officers who had fought on their side in the French and Indian War. Later on, the British gave land to French and German families disturbed by currency problems in the Spanish colony.

Spain built Fort San Gabriel de Manchack on the southern bank of Bayou Manchac. The Spanish government granted lands to Spanish and French families and to French Acadian refugees from Nova Scotia, who had been trickling into the area since 1755.

The British, protecting the edge of a vast territory extending from Bayou Manchac into Canada, countered the Spanish fort by building a more substantial one, Fort New Richmond, on the bluffs of present-day downtown Baton Rouge. From these competitive and contentious roots grew Louisiana's capital city.

By 1776, Fort New Richmond had attracted a few plantations producing indigo, corn, rice, pumpkins, livestock, and wooden staves. British vessels sailing into Bayou Manchac supplied townspeople with all the necessities of life, in turn selling their export goods, quite illegally, to Spanish colonials. Entrepreneurial British merchants made ships into "floating warehouses" stocked with scarce supplies and slowly paraded them up and down the bayou and river.

The Spanish crown, enraged by this contraband trade, used the American Revolution as an excuse to oust the British from West Florida, a territory stretching from Baton Rouge upriver to Natchez, Mississippi, and eastward to present-day Florida. Preparing for war, the Spanish government conscripted seven hundred military-farmers from the Canary Islands. The Spanish governor, Don Bernardo de Galvez, settled one-third of them at the confluence of Bayou Manchac and the Amite River, a swampy, mosquito-riddled habitat unfortunately subject to floods, hurricanes, and fevers.

In 1779, at the height of the American Revolution, Spain declared war on Great Britain. Galvez heard the news weeks before the British forces and assembled a ragtag army to move against British West Florida. Galvez' army was a "league of nations": 170 veteran soldiers, 330 Mexicans and Canary Islanders, and recruits including 80 free blacks and mulattoes,

In the 1840s, French Creole plantations like Magnolia Mound were joined by the grand antebellum homes for which the South is famous. These stately, columned mansions were the "big houses" to the huge sugar plantations in South Louisiana and the large cotton plantations on higher ground north of Baton Rouge. *Photo by Philip Gould*

seven American volunteers, 600 inhabitants of the downriver German and Acadian coasts, and 160 Indians picked up along the way.

The little army quickly captured Fort Bute on Bayou Manchac and moved on to Fort New Richmond in Baton Rouge. Galvez fired artillery from atop an Indian mound, and the British surrendered in less than a day, thus ending English domination of Baton Rouge and ushering in two decades of Spanish rule. The first Battle of Baton Rouge was the only battle of the American Revolution fought outside the thirteen colonies. It was also the first of three battles fought in different wars, a dubious distinction probably unmatched in America.

The Spanish government, although less democratic than the British, was nevertheless generous and mild. Free land grants were available to any comer, and government documents were kept in Spanish, French, and English. Increasing numbers of French settlers arrived, attracted in part by Spanish Catholicism, the only religion that could be practiced in public.

In 1809, a traveler walking along the Baton Rouge riverfront passed houses, inns, and shops selling bread, tobacco, pumpkins, and cheap rum made at nearby sugar plantations. While sharing a bowl of gumbo with other gentlemen at Madame LeGendre's hospitable inn, the traveler concluded that the village of Baton Rouge was a "right French one."

In fact, it was much more cosmopolitan. Beyond Front Street, many of the Bayou Manchac settlers had migrated into town (now called Fort San Carlos). The population of 1,463 people included French, Spanish, Acadians, Canary Islanders, Creoles, Germans, African slaves, free people of color, Indians, English, and Scotch-Irish. By that time, all of the professions and trades were represented here. The wealthy could purchase any type of finery—from silks, ribbons, and hair powders, to books, stationery, and imported wines.

Despite the mildness of Spanish rule, Englishmen were forced to take an oath of loyalty to the Spanish king. Many sold their lands to the crown and departed. The 1803 Louisiana Purchase, which included the Spanish Isle of Orleans, left West Florida a Latin enclave surrounded by Americans. The political climate worsened as time passed and the Spanish granted rich plantation lands to pioneers from Kentucky, Virginia, and Tennessee. The pioneers, floating downriver on flatboats loaded with exports to sell in New Orleans, admired the plantation lands north of Fort San Carlos and returned to settle there. These independent Americans resented Spanish rule and fomented revolution.

On September 22, 1810, around seventy-five calvarymen slipped into Fort San Carlos and disarmed the sleeping guards. The flag of the Republic of West Florida, a blue field with a white star, flew over Baton Rouge until December 10, when the American governor of the Orleans Territory rode into the fort and sent up the U.S. flag of fifteen stars and fifteen stripes.

The colonial period ended as the river swept away the Spanish and British forts on Bayou Manchac. Left behind was a gumbo of international cultures richly flavoring the region with their art, music, food, festivals, and religious traditions.

What the city's diverse cultures held in common was a longing for progress, voiced in cheery shouts at the 1812 arrival of the smoke-belching steamboat, the New Orleans. It appeared to be a novelty, but ushered in almost four decades of lush prosperity in the antebellum South.

Wealthy planters hosted social gatherings for the well-to-do and traveled to New Orleans for the opera, theatre, balls, and assemblies. Steamboat companies of actors, singers, and comedians arrived to entertain the citizens of Baton Rouge, and in their wake came state fairs, circuses, concerts, and revivals.

Baton Rouge's edge on trade was visible on the riverfront, where mercantile stores, warehouses, inns, and taverns crowded together in a row. The town's busy prosperity was a welcome sight to U.S. soldiers arriving here in 1819. With Spain still holding Texas and Mexico, Baton Rouge was the southwestern-most frontier of the United States and the perfect location for a military post. The U.S. government began construction on the Pentagon Barracks, built next to the site of the old star-shaped fort that had been used by the British and Spanish. One of the buildings of the U.S. Arsenal, constructed in 1835 as part of that complex, may be seen today on the grounds of the new State Capitol.

Steamboat pilot Samuel Clemens, better known as Mark Twain, dubbed the original neo-Gothic state capitol a "sham castle." Today, the building is a popular site for tourists, and houses the Center for Political and Governmental History. *Photo by Philip Gould*

Social life revolved around the post, and many young captains and lieutenants married Baton Rouge belles. As Charles East, author and historian, points out, there were Yankee officers in Baton Rouge families before the Civil War. "When the war came," he notes, "Baton Rouge was terribly sympathetic to the Union. For thirty years, it had rubbed shoulders with the U.S. Army."

Famous soldiers and statesmen served at the post, most notably Zachary Taylor, known as "Old Rough and Ready," the hero of the Mexican War. Taylor and his wife lived in a dilapidated cottage overlooking the river. Steamboat passengers cheered as they passed, and when boats docked to unload cargo, people walked up the hill to shake hands and talk with the general.

A delightful old story concerns Taylor's reluctance, as was the custom, to pay postage on incoming letters. One day, he had so much mail that he refused angrily to pay and stomped home. Friends convinced him that his mail might contain important news, so he returned to the post office and picked it up. One letter announced his election as the twelfth president of the United States. General Taylor was inaugurated in 1849, but died the following year.

By that time, plantation wealth had transformed Baton Rouge from a sleepy village into a bustling, wide-awake town. As early as 1822, 83 steamboats, 174 barges and 441 flatboats visited the riverside wharves. Workers busily loaded cotton bales, sugar, tobacco hogsheads and many other area exports into steamers bound for the port of New Orleans.

The old capital building was renovated in the 1880s, replacing the burnt-out interior with an impressive spiraling, cast-iron staircase and a stained glass dome. *Photo by Philip Gould*

Louisiana was the "sugar bowl" of America and soon became its "cotton bowl." Baton Rouge stood at the center of a vast plantation economy built on the riverbanks from Natchez to New Orleans. In 1833, New Orleans exports reached $37 million, of which $20 million was in Louisiana products, mainly sugarcane. By 1860, port receipts in New Orleans exceeded $185 million, of which more than $109 million was in cotton.

The wealth of the antebellum era spilled over into the river town, where two-story homes with wrap-around verandas lined the shady downtown streets. Horses clopped along dirt roads past public buildings and brick businesses. Several old homes and offices still stand today, including the 1837 Warden's House, from which prisoners sold tools, plows, molasses, barrels, and clothing.

The Civil War rolled into Baton Rouge and ripped it to pieces. Many citizens considered slavery a moral evil and an economic albatross hanging around the South's neck. *Photo by Philip Gould*

From 1840 to 1850, Baton Rouge's population nearly doubled from 2,200 to 4,000; in the same period, the parish population in the countryside soared from 5,800 to 16,000. With progress and prosperity came two pivotal events: the 1846 designation of Baton Rouge as Louisiana's state capital and the construction of its statehouse.

DeBow's Review, a popular magazine of the time, described the State Capitol as "gloomy and peculiar." Baton Rougeans paid no heed. The lovely, neo-Gothic building stood proudly on a hill overlooking the river and did, in fact, resemble a medieval castle. In 1850, upon completion of the building, the state's lawmakers settled into spacious upstairs chambers of the House and Senate.

In January 1861, the Louisiana secession convention met in the elegant State Capitol, voted to secede and two months later joined the Confederacy. Two years later, Union soldiers quartered in the building lit a cooking fire that later blazed out of control and left the capitol a gutted ruin. It was a symbol of the wreckage to come as the Civil War rolled into Baton Rouge and ripped it to pieces. Many citizens considered slavery a moral evil and an economic albatross hanging around the South's neck. Others were pro-Union: There was a deathly silence when secessionists pulled down the U.S. flag and it floated slowly to the ground. Most Louisianians favored secession, however. Slavery was an economic institution: In 1850, two-thirds of America's millionaires lived on the river road from Natchez, Mississippi, to New Orleans.

In April 1862, rumors of the capture of New Orleans terrified Baton Rougeans, who realized that Union control of the river would mean the capture of Baton Rouge as well. Many townspeople fled to the homes of relatives in the countryside, while others scurried to the commons to burn cotton bales heaped there and on a flatboat in the river. A fleet of federal gunboats arrived in May, but stood a silent vigil until Union soldiers rowing to shore with their laundry were killed by guerilla cavalrymen. The Essex shelled Baton Rouge from the river and federal troops marched into the wreckage. Officers were quartered in the Barracks and Arsenal, while soldiers took over the State Capitol and pitched thousands of tents on the grounds of the Louisiana State Penitentiary.

The Confederate commander, General John C. Breckinridge, attempted to retake Baton Rouge on August 5. Union and Confederate troops fought a bloody battle on the eastern outskirts of the town, with bullets richocheting off tombstones in Magnolia Cemetery. The Confederates forced the federal troops toward the river, expecting support from the ironclad C.S.S. Arkansas, but support never came. The Arkansas developed engine trouble just north of the city and was scuttled in Baton Rouge. The Essex fired on the Confederates, forcing them to withdraw. The rattled Union commander evacuated his garrison, making the battle a Rebel victory with each side losing about four hundred men. But the price was dear.

In the days following the battle, Union troops returned and torched one-third of the city to clear a firing lane in case of a second Confederate attack. Instead, the Confederate troops marched on to reinforce nearby Port Hudson, where big guns shelled Union vessels from high, wooded bluffs. Port Hudson was captured shortly after the July 1863 fall of Vicksburg, enabling the Federals to take control of the river and split the Confederacy in two. A commemorative area at Port

Slavery was an economic institution. At the end of the Civil War, the inhumanity of slavery had brought the city to its knees. Without slave labor, commerce ground to a halt. *Photo by Philip Gould*

Huey P. Long, one of the most powerful politicians in Louisiana history, burst into the spotlight in the mid-1920s. After all these years, Louisiana is still sharply divided into two factions, pro-Long and anti-Long.
Photo by Philip Gould

Hudson, complete with walkways, a tower, and museum, recalls this battle, the longest siege in American history.

Union troops left Baton Rouge shortly after the end of the war in April 1865. Upwards of seventeen thousand soldiers had occupied the town of six thousand people, many of whom lived under martial law for four years. The city's sorrow and loss was recorded in a diary kept by Sarah Morgan, a gifted young writer, musician and daughter of a judge. "A Confederate Girl's Diary," published after her death, vividly captures the devastation of the Civil War. After it ended, veterans and townspeople returned to homes that were destroyed or occupied by others. Gone was Baton Rouge as they had known it.

The inhumanity of slavery had brought the city to its knees, and atonement was not a pretty sight. Without slave labor, commerce ground to a halt. In the countryside, planters rolled up their sleeves and went to work in the fields, but markets were disrupted and recovery was slow. Baton Rouge suffered poverty, crime, racial conflict, and political strife, yet in the midst of these troubles were the seeds of recovery—the stalwart people of the city. Epidemics, floods, hurricanes, and now a third battle, a war among kinsmen, had tested their mettle. They were survivors. To the five flags of France, Britain, Spain, the Republic of West Florida, and the United States were now added the briefly flown secessionist flag of Louisiana and the flag of the Confederacy.

The return of the Stars and Stripes revived hopes for peace and unity. Within a few years, businesses began to repair buildings while churches and civic clubs organized benefits, fairs, and balls. Baton Rougeans formed a baseball team, the first "Red Sticks," and built a new racetrack. The Louisiana State Seminary of Learning moved to town in 1869 and to the old U.S. Arsenal grounds in 1886. Soon, the Pentagon Barracks was home to a state university fondly referred to as the "Old War Skule."

In the 1880s, to the delight of townspeople, the Louisiana legislature moved the state capital back to Baton Rouge from New Orleans, where the federals held it during the Civil War and Reconstruction. Home to owls and rubbish for two decades, the interior of the burnt-out statehouse was rebuilt with a spiraling, cast iron staircase and a stained glass dome.

Steamboats still plied the river's waters, but railroads whistled progress into town. On the evening of December 15, 1883, a crowd was on hand to meet the first train, and by the end of 1884, a line to Memphis was completed. Baton Rouge's first depot was about where the Louisiana Arts and Science Center, the third depot, is located now. The New Orleans and Mississippi Valley Railroad connected Baton Rouge with commerce across America, and the result was rapid growth. Between 1860 and 1890, the town's population nearly doubled to 10,478, with a total of 25,922 people living in the parish.

While retaining its small town atmosphere, Baton Rouge was fast becoming a city. Just before the turn of the century, mule-drawn carts were replaced by electric streetcars and a progressive mayor won a bond issue for paved streets, new schools, a hospital site, and a new city hall. The times were a'changin' and especially after 1901, when Louisiana struck oil and in 1916, struck gas.

In 1909, Standard Oil built a refinery north of town and shifted the city's economic base from agriculture to manufacturing. A local newspaper, the ***State-Times***, wrote that construction wages would equal "at least two-thirds of the total money value of the entire cotton crop of East Baton Rouge for the year." Almost overnight, Baton Rouge was transformed from a town catering to farmers into an industrial city catering to one of the world's most powerful corporations.

Huey P. Long, one of the most powerful politicians in Louisiana history, burst into the spotlight in the mid-1920s. By levying taxes and enforcing laws on big corporations, Standard Oil among them, Long won enough popular support to change the course of American history. Baton Rouge is rich with stories about the self-styled Kingfish, whose remains are buried under a massive statue on the grounds of his State Capitol building. After all these years, Louisiana is still divided into two factions, pro-Long and anti-Long.

Originally a patent medicine salesman, the charismatic lawyer, governor and U.S. senator frequently excited strong emotions in people, who viewed him as a dictator, demagogue, savior, or good Samaritan, depending on their personal politics. But whether they loved him or hated him, the fact remains: Long kept his word to the poor, unemployed, and undereducated people of Louisiana and changed their lives for the better. During the Great Depression, his "Share Our Wealth" program struck a responsive chord in millions of Americans. Had he lived a few more years, he might well have become Baton Rouge's second U.S. president.

In 1935, Long was shot down in the marble halls of his State Capitol. Some believe had he lived a few more years, Long would have become Baton Rouge's second U.S. president.
Photo by Philip Gould

Long's platform in his 1928 gubernatorial campaign was "Every Man a King," and when he won the election, at age 34, he shared the crown. During the grim years of the Great Depression, he launched a massive public works program that provided badly needed jobs and advanced Louisiana into the 20th century. In Baton Rouge, he built the first bridge across the river and a governor's mansion designed like the White House: He wanted to be familiar with its layout, he said, when he became president. In 1932, fearful of assassination and always surrounded by bodyguards, he took an apartment in his new, 34-story State Capitol building, still the tallest in America. Its lovely sculptures pay tribute to the pioneers who settled the state and the patriots who fought its battles over the years.

The question lingering in Louisiana is whether Long's means justified the ends. The crown prince of verbal volleys and sizzling sarcasm, he accomplished his public improvements program by absorbing the ruling political hierarchy and erecting his own machine. Seemingly aware that his time was limited, he was ruthless in taking shortcuts to get things done. Nonetheless, he was a brilliant political strategist and the high comedy created by his dagger-like wit endeared him to the common man and won over many of his enemies.

Long's capers fill the pages of many books and the best of them recount his love affair with Louisiana State University. While serving as governor, he concocted ways to fund LSU, which began to blossom in those years. Here and in other cities, he led the LSU Fighting Tigers Marching Band in parades, striding between the drum majors and waving his baton, and he fueled the football fever still raging in Baton Rouge. At one LSU football game, he walked up to an official at halftime and told him firmly, "Now I want to say one thing. As governor, I protest your calls. I don't mind you penalizing LSU, but penalize us in midfield. Don't do it when we get down to the goal line."

Elected to the U.S. Senate in 1932, Long continued to rule Louisiana politics with an iron hand. When Huey blew into town, people knew that a special session of the legislature was brewing. While concentrating more and more power in the hands of the state, he took the U.S. Senate by storm, injecting the issue of concentrated wealth—his favorite topic—and introducing a bold proposal to redistribute the country's riches by taxation. Still the champion of the poor and enemy of the rich, the maverick senator helped elect Franklin D. Roosevelt president but broke with him when Roosevelt, attempting to curb Long's growing power, granted federal jobs to Huey's enemies in Louisiana. Long retaliated by using radio to promote his "Share Our Wealth" program and by encouraging people to form Share Our Wealth clubs across America. Millions joined these clubs and their popularity prompted Roosevelt, in 1935, to announce plans to alleviate social unrest through a wider distribution of wealth.

The same year, Long was shot down in the marble halls of his State Capitol, which still bears traces of one bullet hole. The assassin was a brilliant, idealistic young physician, Carl Weiss, who perceived Long as a mad dictator and was angry about a relative of his wife's who would have been gerrymandered out of a judicial seat. Various myths have cast doubt on the identity of the murderer, especially in recent years, but it is unlikely that any other suspect will be found.

Huey's younger brother, Earl, known as "Uncle Earl" and "The Last of the Red Hot Poppas," was an equally flamboyant figure and spellbinding stump orator. But there was more to Uncle Earl than the countrified witticisms for which he is best known. Three times the governor of the state, he shared Huey's concern for poor people and minorities. In the 1950s, he influenced registrars in Louisiana parishes to enfranchise black people, who were kept from voting by unfair literacy tests. His famous mental breakdown occurred while fighting in the legislature for a bill to stop the purging of black people from voter rolls.

Huey's program of education and social welfare uplifted African-Americans, but it was Earl who, in advance of the Civil Rights Act, brought the segregation issue into the open across Louisiana and the South.

In the 1960s, racial differences brought conflict to the city once again, but people reached out to each other and gathered in private homes to bridge cultural gaps. The effort continues today in community-building programs initiated by parish government, churches, and peace

groups. The 1960s and 1970s also marked a cultural renaissance for native people and the Cajuns of Louisiana, who began to regain their languages and traditions at this time.

Since 1699, despite its struggles, Baton Rouge has been immersed in the French *joie de vivre*, or love of life, that is its legacy. In recent decades, the city's cultural wealth has been enriched by waves of immigrants escaping political conflict in their native countries. Today, people from more than fifty nations live in Baton Rouge, a capital city open and willing to embrace growth and change. Our diversity creates an ever-deepening understanding and acceptance of each other, and, according to John Maginnis, a leading political analyst and author, a more successful economy. With fewer cultural obstacles in the way, the city is better able to develop along economic lines.

Baton Rouge, as the state capital, is a cultural crossroads leading to the best in Louisiana and, in many cases, in America and the world. Our incomparable music, art, food, festivals, natural resources, and open, friendly people are like powerful magnets irresistibly drawing people here from every corner of the world.

Industry, state government, the universities, and a thriving healthcare community futher increase cultural diversity by recruiting top thinkers and researchers from across the U.S. and abroad. Their skills and creative talent yield a vibrant formula that brightens Baton Rouge's horizons: diversity > tolerance > kindness > opportunity. Like a circle, it works just as well in reverse.

The global challenge of the 21st century is to balance the needs of people with those of business, not an easy task for any city and especially for an industrial, commercial, and political hub like Baton Rouge.

And yet, because of our tumultuous colonial history, we have learned a great deal about living and working in harmony with each other and the land.

This is a tricentennial and millennial achievement worth celebrating: The Red Stick, having stirred the currents of history for three hundred years, aspires to be and is working to become a landmark in the progression of human development.

Baton Rouge, as the state capital, is a cultural crossroads leading to the best in Louisiana and, in many cases, in America and the world. *Photo by Philip Gould*

Chapter 2

The "Kingfish" of Commerce

Tourists flock to Louisiana's capital city, enjoying the city's scenic Southern beauty, art galleries, museums, historic attractions, and to try their luck on the two riverboat casinos.
Photo by Philip Gould

Daytime brings hustle and bustle to America's fifth largest tonnage port and 87th largest city. Cars and trucks zoom along interstates and highways transporting forty thousand students to two major universities and fifty thousand workers to government jobs toward the river near the busy downtown.

On the waterfront, the city dock's open arches welcome commerce to the capital city. The Delta Queen, a paddlewheeler moored at the dock, plays a calliope tune that drifts over the levee into the central business district. On weekdays, more than 100,000 people do business in a downtown area made festive by colorful banners and crowds of tourists traipsing into restaurants, art galleries, museums, and historic buildings.

On the river's west bank, a beehive of activity swarms at the Port of Greater Baton Rouge. Longshoremen scurry back and forth on the general cargo docks, heaving forest products, pipe, and molasses into the holds of ships destined for Europe, Australia, the Pacific Rim, and South America. At a midstream handling facility, a boom swings a giant clam bucket of grain from barge to ship.

Downriver at a chemical plant, construction workers click a huge steel pipe into place, while supply trucks roll in and out of guard gates. Parts and tools arrive on time and error-free, efficiently fueling industrial expansions and, in turn, the booming retail and service sectors of the four-parish metro economy.

The "kingfish" moniker, a symbol of power and prestige, is well-deserved by Baton Rouge, since the riches of the river and the state—in people, jobs, and resources—flow into the capital city and boost its thriving economy.
Photo by Philip Gould

No matter where you travel in Baton Rouge, you can't get far from the river. It is a dynamic engine of commerce, streaming past the city, in high water, at the rate of 729,000 cubic feet per second—collecting, building, growing, and churning its way from America's heartland to the Gulf of Mexico. In one way or another, that energy has given rise to Baton Rouge—a hub of Indian trade for thousands of years and today a "kingfish" of commerce.

The "kingfish" moniker, a symbol of power and prestige, is well-deserved by Baton Rouge, since the riches of the river and the state—in people, jobs, and resources—flow into the capital city and boost its thriving economy. With low unemployment, rapid population growth and a high quality of life, as Huey Long "the Kingfish," dreamed, every man can be a king. And with several economic engines holding court, as Huey insisted, no man wears a crown.

John Borland, economic research manager for The Chamber of Greater Baton Rouge, compares the city's economy to a stool held up by four strong legs: state government, the petrochemical industry, health care and medical research, and two major universities: Louisiana State University, the state's flagship,

The Mississippi River is a dynamic engine of commerce in Baton Rouge, streaming past the city, in high water, at the rate of 729,000 cubic feet per second.
Photo by Philip Gould

and Southern University, the largest predominately black university in the nation.

The beauty of the stool metaphor is this: If one of the legs is damaged, it will not tip over. When the price of oil crashed in the 1980s, it triggered an economic downturn along the Gulf Coast and, in some cities, thrust unemployment to 17 percent.

Baton Rouge, supported by its diverse economy, lost only 2.2 percent of its jobs. The city's other economic engines drove it out of the recession, and the lost jobs were regained by 1988. Baton Rouge has been setting employment records since, and that performance is the best in the state.

The capital city, in fact, is one of Louisiana's fastest growing metro areas. The annual growth rate hovers at a consistent 3 percent and at times exceeds 4 percent, compared to a national growth rate of 2 to 2.5 percent.

Baton Rouge is growing incredibly fast. From 1970 to 1998, the parish population increased from 285,000 to nearly 400,000, with a metro population of 576,000, and 675,000 in the nine-parish region served by the Chamber of Commerce. U.S. Census projections through the year 2010 predict a population explosion in Baton Rouge—18 percent by the year 2007—and the city's future as a regional urban center.

Newcomers are attracted here by two powerful magnets: a low unemployment rate of 3.7 percent and a high household income running neck-in-neck with St. Tammany Parish, the frontrunner and a wealthy suburb of New Orleans.

Within the four-parish metropolitan region served by The Chamber of Greater Baton Rouge, thirty-one thousand people work for state government, the single largest employer. Education is the second largest, with the two universities and the parish school system employing upwards of twenty-four thousand people.

The service sector (including health care) at 25.2 percent, and retail trade, at 19.2 percent, account for nearly half of the 296,000 jobs in the metro area. Recently, these sectors have surged in growth, with hotels constructing additional convention and meeting space and several telemarketing companies, hotel reservation centers, and credit card processors

relocating to Baton Rouge. One of the largest telemarketers employs 1,500 people.

While state government, education, and health care stabilize the city's economy, the petrochemical industry is clearly its vital spark. Manufacturing accounts for only 8.5 percent of metro jobs, but three-fourths of these are at industrial plants which pay the highest wages: in 1998, a conservative average of $50,000 per year.

The petrochemical industry, with its direct wages, spinoff jobs, plant expansions, retail purchases, and tax contributions, is the force behind the city's booming economy. Including the Exxon Company, U.S.A., the largest oil refinery in America, and Exxon Chemical Americas, a total of 26 chemical manufacturers in the parish employ 5,100 people at an annual wage of $290 million.

This is the largest and highest-paying concentration of chemical industry payrolls in Louisiana. But direct wages are only a fraction of the petrochemical impact. Exxon Chemical Americas, for example, purchases an annual $300 million in goods from local merchants and pays $14.5 million in state and local taxes and $6.6 million in property taxes.

An additional impact is in spinoff jobs created by the two industries, according to Loren C. Scott, Ph.D. and director of the LSU Division of Economic Development and Forecasting. Within the four-parish metro area, some 12,000 jobs at chemical plants multiply into 72,000 jobs in the service and retail sectors of the economy. Using a conservative economic multiplier, some 2,100 jobs in the petrochemical industry add up to 11,500 jobs in related businesses.

Business and industry employ productive workforces committed to refining their skills. The high standards of quality brought about by the Quality Improvement Process and ISO 9002 have echoed into the Baton Rouge corporate sector, where lower costs and higher

The petrochemical industry is the force behind the city's booming economy.
Photo by Philip Gould

The river's inland waterway system is perfectly suited to barge traffic. Port cargoes range from grain, sugar, cotton, and molasses to bauxite, coal, alloys, petroleum coke, fertilizers, and minerals.
Photo by Philip Gould

productivity make profits soar and give companies an edge in the global marketplace.

So deeply invested in the Quality movement, Baton Rouge is at the forefront of a corporate culture shift to competition through cooperation: that is, the drawing forth the leadership skills and employee talents for their own benefit and that of their employers. Today, entrepreneurial trainers are taking the industrial sector beyond the principles of quality management into innovative, hands-on teamwork training. Baton Rouge business and industry are fine-tuning operations efficiency, corporate communications, and employee teams devoted to doing more at a lower cost. Bolstered by their local contracts, service and supply companies are branching out across the Gulf Coast and are in high demand internationally.

Baton Rouge's dependable, efficient workforce is a bonus to industry and the world economy, individually and collectively since the state's 100 chemical plants export one-third of their sales to foreigners and enhance America's balance of trade. People work hard here and very well.

Only bright horizons lie ahead for the petrochemical industry. Louisiana is the second highest producer of natural gas and third highest producer of crude oil within the fifty states. Today, oil and gas extraction in the Gulf of Mexico is busier than it's been in over a decade and is expected to increase the supply of industrial raw materials, which will further lower prices. Still more promising for industry is the lowering of international trade barriers by the NAFTA and GATT treaties. As the economies of Mexico and Canada grow stronger, heightened trade will increase industrial expansions and continue to bring high-skill, high-paying jobs to Baton Rouge.

Industrial expansions are consistent and ongoing. Plants are constantly modernized and updated for efficiency and environmental controls. In the Baton Rouge metro area, announced industrial investment in 1998 was $1.2 billion. By the year 2002, the Baton Rouge metro area is expected to announce an additional $5 billion in industrial investment. Industries will expand along the river corridor from Baton Rouge to New Orleans for the same reasons that brought them here: oil and gas as raw materials, the cooling power of the river, and ready access to a vast inland waterway system and ocean lanes at the Gulf of Mexico. Seven cargo and commodity handling facilities at the Port of Greater Baton Rouge expedite industrial shipping, Louisiana products, and domestic and international commerce.

Ships flying the flags of thirty nations sail into the 85-mile jurisdiction of the Port of Greater Baton Rouge, the farthest inland deepwater port on the Mississippi. It is the fifth largest tonnage port in America, handling 84 million short tons of cargo each year, including industrial imports and exports. A 45-foot-draft channel accommodates ocean-going vessels sailing in from the Gulf of Mexico and back out to the ocean trade lanes of Latin America, Europe, the Far East, and the world.

The river's inland waterway system is perfectly suited to barge traffic. Tugs and towboats haul barges downstream to offload here on ships sailing through the Port of New Orleans to overseas destinations. At Baton Rouge, the barges turn easily into the Gulf Intracoastal Waterway flowing east-west from Houston to Mobile. Heading north, they transport goods into America's heartland.

Port cargoes range from grain, sugar, cotton, and molasses to bauxite, coal, alloys, petroleum coke, fertilizers, and minerals. The general cargo dock has a continuous wharf of three thousand feet and a transit shed with a half million square feet of storage space. A new Inland Marine Terminal is an intermodal facility and a vital transit center accessible by road, rail, water, and air.

Stevedores, longshoremen, and dock workers handle a throng of activity at the port, which employs three thousand people and creates an economic impact of $70 million in a four-parish area. Port-related activities result in $340 million in direct spending and yield $10 million in taxes within the port's jurisdiction.

Tourism is an important industry in the eight-parish area. The state capitol building, with its intricate carvings, draws many visitors for an appreciation of both art and history.
Photo by Philip Gould

Baton Rouge's excellent inland transportation system complements shipping activities. Products travel on a modern system of rail lines as well as a corridor of highways crisscrossing America. Interstate 10 stretches east-west from Jacksonville, Florida, to Los Angeles, while I-55, off I-12, links directly with Chicago. This tightly networked highway system elevates Baton Rouge to the rank of a major trucking center.

Tourists travel the same routes into the capital city, a gateway to Louisiana's cultural riches and a destination in itself. Visitors enjoy the city's scenic Southern beauty, art galleries, museums, and historic attractions, two riverboat casinos presenting festivals and concerts year-round, exciting sports competitions, and easy access to tourist attractions in other parts of the state. As of 1997, tourism was a $553 million industry in an eight-parish area, with conventions at $41 million in 1998. Both industries are on the rise, due to the aggressive marketing efforts of the Baton Rouge Area Convention & Visitors Bureau.

The dollar spin-off of this economic growth, spilling over into jobs, retail sales, and tax revenues, is sprucing up the city and changing its skyline. A fast-track $61 million construction program at the Baton Rouge Metropolitan Airport, north of town, anticipates future population growth and the airport's destiny as a cargo hub. On the south side of the city, the new Mall of Louisiana, at 1.3 million square feet, rivals in size the east-lying Mall at Cortana, the largest shopping center in the South. Both make Baton Rouge a regional magnet for retail stores and metro shoppers. The new Baton Rouge Community College in mid-city, a $15 million investment, offers a two-year associate degree in art, science, and business and trains adults for re-entry into the city's rapidly expanding workforce.

The LSU band helped kick off the gala celebration marking the opening of the new Mall of Louisiana. The mall offers 1.3 million square feet of shopping, dining, and entertainment space.
Photo by Philip Gould

Perhaps the most visible sign of city progress is a massive construction program in the downtown area. Downtown revitalization efforts include the construction of five state buildings in a 250-acre complex, Capitol Park. The $160 million program, located at the north edge of the Central Business District, will bring three thousand state employees

Within the four-parish metropolitan region served by The Chamber of Greater Baton Rouge, thirty-one thousand people work for state government, the single largest employer.

Photo by Philip Gould

back to the downtown area. The lobbies of each building, scheduled for completion by the year 2003, will depict the state's history.

With Capitol Park and blueprints on a $6.8 million, tilted-dome planetarium and space theater, the only one of its kind in America, an ambitious revitalization effort is underway downtown. It began in 1987 with the creation of the Downtown Development District, a political subdivision of the state that is funded by a 10 millage downtown property tax.

Over the past decade, the DDD has helped stimulate $400 million in development and redevelopment. Included is a $30 million expansion of the exhibition hall and arena at the Riverside Centroplex, the city's civic and convention center. All of this activity has sparked a restoration renaissance in historic buildings and two adjacent neighborhoods, the 1805 Spanish Town and the 1806 Beauregard Town.

Committed to building community, many thousands of people contribute their time and talents to the economic vitality of Baton Rouge, from festival organizers and civic volunteers devising a downtown arts district to Create Baton Rouge, a cultural plan for the year 2000. Complementary efforts are made by volunteers of the Baton Rouge Sports Foundation, which attracted the Baton Rouge Kingfish, a professional indoor ice hockey team playing home games to sellout crowds at the Riverside Centroplex.

Weaving these efforts into a seamless whole is Plan Baton Rouge, a full-scale public/private initiative funded by the non-profit Baton Rouge Area Foundation, the city, and the state. A collective effort to rejuvenate the city center through master planning, Plan Baton Rouge is being fashioned out of the hopes and dreams of citizens and forged by a world class urban planning firm.

Quality of life is and always has been a preoccupation of Baton Rougeans—and not just for their own benefit. Some $76 million in grants attracted by the two universities enhance basic research and the core industries of Louisiana: agriculture, the petrochemical industry, and tourism. In East Baton Rouge Parish, agriculture is only a $75 million industry, but it's big business in the rest of the state.

The Louisiana Agricultural Experiment Station, a division of the LSU Agricultural Center, supports every commodity produced in Louisiana with a $40 million budget and seventeen research stations spread across the state. Scientists study experimental varieties of cotton and sugarcane, still the primary row crops, along with crawfish, catfish, and alligators raised in ponds. The experiment stations

also research vegetables and ornamentals like sweet potatoes, the primary horticultural crop, and forestry, Louisiana's number one export crop.

The two universities, the petrochemical industry, LSU Medical School, and area medical centers are the basis of a vibrant research and development sector in Baton Rouge. The Pennington Biomedical Research Center and the Center for Advanced Microstructures and Devices (CAMD) are both affiliated with LSU. Scientists focused on nutrition, diabetes and obesity research at the Pennington Center host international conferences and attract visiting scientists as well as an annual $17 million in federal and private research grants.

The Center for Advanced Microstructures and Devices attracts international attention with a $20 million electron storage ring emitting high-intensity X-rays used for basic research in physics, chemistry, and other sciences. CAM-D is best known for microfabrication activities producing micromachines, microsensors, and other tiny devices for governmental and industrial customers like IBM and Honeywell. CAM-D's 126-acre research park will ultimately attract more high-tech businesses to Baton Rouge.

Science, industry, business, and government work hand in hand for economic development in Baton Rouge and Louisiana. At the same time, progressive thinking guides the city, milestone by milestone, out of socio-economic struggle into harmony. In every case, this bold leadership paves the way for progress in the twenty-first century.

While the mayor-president implements a regional economic development plan emphasizing the growing technology base in Baton Rouge, his community development team coordinates town meetings on everything from air quality and services for children, to community policing, racism, and public education.

The Chamber of Greater Baton Rouge addresses the concerns of the business community with vision and timely projects. Among them are a leadership program for burgeoning city leaders; the Service Corps of Retired Executives (SCORE), which gives free financial guidance to aspiring business people; a strong, consistent focus on public education; and a workforce development program connecting youths with entry-level training jobs made available by local businesses.

Baton Rouge is indeed the "kingfish" of commerce—vigorous, flourishing, and immensely successful in its people and resources.

Science, industry, business, and government work hand in hand for economic development in Baton Rouge and Louisiana. *Photo by Philip Gould*

The Chamber's John Borland says it best: "We have an enormous potential for growth— the education, intelligence, and wealth is here. Anything is possible. With the imagination of its leaders and people, Baton Rouge can determine its own destiny." ✤

Chapter 3

City of Cultures, City of Character

A bank teller spends Saturday afternoon reading to a youngster in need of a Big Buddy. Nurses originate a program giving free immunizations to fifth-graders in a four-parish area. Students plant trees with Baton Rouge Green, and retirees sort cans of food for the Greater Baton Rouge Food Bank. Retired executives teach new business owners management skills, and plant workers, on their days off, wire schools for computers then show kids how to use them.

Building a city with character takes all kinds and lots of kindness, the two best things about Baton Rouge. A wide-ranging cultural diversity and the innate generosity of the people make this a warm, welcoming place to live.

It's an indisputable fact that Baton Rougeans are quick to extend a helping hand to people in need. Compassionate folks, by the thousands, contribute their time, talent, and treasure to worth causes like the Food Bank and the St. Vincent de Paul Dining Room. As in the old days, some build homes for homeless families through Habitat for Humanity, while others repair old houses and entire neighborhoods through Fix-Up! Mid City, one of several initiative (including Volunteer Baton Rouge! and Create Baton Rouge!) that carry the excitement of giving in their exclamation points.

The Italian American Society starts preparing cakes and cookies for its St. Joseph's Altar in January. The goodies, along with fresh fruit and vegetables, are given away each March 19, the annual feast day of St. Joseph, patron saint of the Italians and the poor.
Photo by Philip Gould

Ecumenical services bring together black and white churches belonging to the Greater Baton Rouge Federation of Churches and Synagogues. The Federation was established in 1986 to bring people of diverse faiths together to work on mutual understanding and to be a blessing to the community.
Photo by Philip Gould

Some of this generosity comes, no doubt, from the city's legacy of spirituality. Houses of worship became the center of social activities in the 1790s, when St. Joseph's Church, now Cathedral, delivered its sermons in French. Beautiful churches like St. James Episcopal were lovingly built downtown, and by 1859, with the formation of the Jewish Congregation B'Nai Israel, all major religions had a home in Baton Rouge. Services are held today in English, Spanish, Chinese, and Vietnamese. The city also has Hindu and Buddhist temples.

The people featured in this chapter are just a few of many who give of themselves in great and small ways. Still, they are a fair measure of Baton Rougeans, remarkably good-natured, well-intentioned people willing to work together in partnership to lift one and all toward a happier, more prosperous future.

Eddie "Walking Shadow" Rainwater shares the heritage and history of his Native American people with new generations.

Photo by Philip Gould

Walking Shadow Walks Tall

Eddie "Walking Shadow" Rainwater hunts as quietly as a shadow in the woods and swamps of Louisiana, as did his ancestors thousands of years ago. During Andrew Jackson's Trail of Tears, an 1813-1854 government relocation of tribes east of the Mississippi River, the majority of Louisiana's native people were massacred or lost their lands, languages, and ancient cultures. Chief Walking Shadow's ancestors managed to escape back into the wilderness they knew so well.

Like many native people, Walking Shadow ignored his Indian heritage until the 1960s. At that time, he claimed his blood lineage as a Choctaw chief and, with a small band of Indian Angels, persuaded family clans across the state to reclaim their identities, too.

Because of Chief Rainwater's activism, his own tribe, the Louisiana Band of Choctaw, and four others (the Houma, Chitimacha, Tunica, and Alabama Coushatta) are gathering the fragments of their civilizations and building them anew. They have regained their self-respect, dignity, and state or federal recognition, which brings with it the hope of land.

The chief, now in his seventies, still teaches people about the Great Spirit and living in harmony with nature. He brings Indian artifacts, drums, and a teepee to schools and, back at home, shares his medicine wheel and Indian village with visitors.

The Indian Angels, of which he is the only survivor, were single-handedly responsible for the cultural renaissance among Louisiana's native people, seen today in pow-wows, dance competitions, and educational events. In these outreach efforts, they are attempting to forge alliances among the state's tribes while fostering unity among all people: red, yellow, black, and white.

The Nguyens provide a link for Vietnamese refugees searching for family ties, and welcome Asian newcomers to Baton Rouge with assistance in getting settled and starting a business.
Photo by Philip Gould

The Nguyen Family: Rescuing Survivors

The Vietnam War, with all of its horror and death, ravaged the Nguyen family from 1963 until 1975, when Loan, Yduc and twenty relatives escaped Saigon only two days before the country fell to Communism.

They would have been killed by the Viet Cong, since Yduc, a doctor serving on the front lines, was politically involved as a councilman and assisted his wife, Loan, a lawyer, in rescuing young war victims. Loan argued in court for juveniles arrested for stealing food, Yduc helped them get off drugs, and both taught them ways to earn money, often by shining shoes.

The Nguyens fled Saigon amidst a volley of bullets and flew from their country on a U.S. military plane. Yduc was working in an Army hospital when a Vacherie, Louisiana, medical doctor, Roland Waguespack, volunteered to sponsor his family. The Nguyens studied English at LSU and settled in Baton Rouge to raise a family and, like Catholic Social Services, help other refugees find their way home. Today, they do what they did in Vietnam and what Americans did for them. Working through associations, they raise funds for community causes, welcome Asian newcomers to the city and help them get started in business.

Loan, an accountant with the school system, serves on the advisory board of Woman's Hospital, works with the Catholic Vietnamese church, and mothers five adult children working as a global job recruiter, designer, medical doctor, chiropractor, and college student. Yduc, a physician at the Baton Rouge Mental Health Center, is president of the Vietnamese Community Association and the Asian American Association of South Louisiana, Inc. He is also a valued member of the Baton Rouge Center for World Affairs.

There are about eighty Vietnamese businesses in Baton Rouge. The Asian American Association, of which most are part, includes people from India, China, Japan, Laos, the Philippines, Pakistan, Korea, Sri Lanka, and Iran. ✦

Lawrence and Gerri Hobdy have created award-winning programs geared toward educating children about such social issues as drug prevention, and teaching African-American children about the riches of their cultural and artistic heritage. They and their children make their home in Baton Rouge. *Photo by Philip Gould*

Making a Difference: Gerri and Lawrence Hobdy

Gerri and Lawrence Hobdy met in New Orleans, where Gerri was studying theater and communications at Dillard University and Lawrence was in his second year of medical school at Tulane. Their mutual love for the arts, humanities, and family life led them into marriage and careers in Baton Rouge.

A Harvard graduate, Lawrence wanted time for a family and switched from medicine to the field of substance abuse. In 1993, after serving as a counselor, administrator, speaker, and workshop leader, he opened a consulting business serving substance abuse and emotional health centers in fifteen states.

Gerri obtained a master's degree at the University of New Orleans, taught theater at Southern University, and worked in community arts development for the local Arts Council and the state Division of the Arts. In 1992, she was appointed secretary of the Louisiana Office of Cultural Development, which oversees the arts and humanities, archaeology, and historic preservation.

Jointly and in solido, the Hobdys have made waves in Baton Rouge. Their drug prevention play, "Barking Back," won a state award, while "Out Loud!", a five-year program in elementary schools, changed the lives of African-American children by exposing them to local African-American artists possessing cultural brilliance.

As secretary of the Office of Cultural Development, Gerri persuaded the Louisiana Legislature to allot a 50-cent per capita assessment for community-based programs across the state; these exciting programs have triggered an annual $7 million arts and humanities renaissance in Louisiana. Boosting that economic impact is Gerri's Main Street U.S.A. program, which is transforming Louisiana's decrepit historic buildings into thriving museums, antique malls, mercantile stores, and cultural facilities. An initial $200,000 state investment has leveraged more than two thousand jobs and $75 million in 1,000 new businesses in historic buildings being rehabbed across the state.

The family's humanitarian endeavors are local as well as statewide and national. Gerri, a founding member of the city's chapter of 100 Black Women, enjoys arts and family-based organizations like La Capitale Links and Jack and Jill. Lawrence works with 100 Black Men on projects like anti-violence billboard campaigns, youth mentoring, and Project Excel, which tracks students and guarantees them education scholarships.

The Hobdys are parents to Daniel, Donovan, and Judy, as well as countless numbers of kids who will mimic their depth of character.

Since her teenage years, lifetime Baton Rougean Mary Frey Eaton has made volunteering her time and talents to the betterment of the city and state a top priority. *Photo by Philip Gould*

Mary Frey Eaton: Leadership and Good Government

Words like "honor" and "public service" are a first language to Mary Frey Eaton, a lifelong volunteer, mayor pro tem and member of the Metropolitan Council. The daughter of LSU's second economics professor, she grew up in the 1920s playing on the old university campus and future grounds of the State Capitol.

As a teenager, Mary sold American Legion poppies on Armistice Day and, during World War II, headed a Bundles for Britain project at Baton Rouge High School. She knitted the caps and sweaters left unfinished by other girls and could have envisioned her future in them. Working through the arts, education, and government, she would weave her life into the very fabric of her city.

While studying history and English at LSU, she met Lewis Eaton, Jr., a football player who became a building contractor and prominent civic leader. He took a seat on the first Metropolitan Council, served in the Louisiana Senate, and helped organize United Way, the Public Affairs Research Council, and Council for A Better Louisiana.

The mother of five, Mary served as president of the Junior League of Baton Rouge, chaired the Nearly Nu Store for years and trained hundreds of women in effective leadership and community responsibility. "I have seen women blossom and make tremendous contributions to this community," she says proudly.

She was a good example for them. She led church projects to provide health kits to prisons, teach clerical skills to unemployed women, and foster interracial harmony. After her husband's death in 1977, civic leaders persuaded her to become the first president of the Arts Council's Community Fund for the Arts. With her guidance, business supported the arts program. It is still successful today.

As a member of CHAMPAC, a Chamber of Commerce program, Eaton encouraged others to enter politics. In 1988, she practiced what she preached and ran for the Metro Council, winning by a landslide. During her third term, she was elected mayor pro tem.

The epitome of a "steel magnolia," this strong, gracious woman has beautified the lives of countless people. Today, she is helping to "grow" the city's future for generations to come. As for her contributions, she says simply, "This is where I am, and where you are, you serve." ⚜

Frank Bonifay, Kermit Braud, and Jim Ragland joined forces to create the non-profit Bluff Swamp Wildlife Refuge, preserving 901 acres of land now being restored as a wildlife refuge.
Photo by Philip Gould

Saving Louisiana's Roots and Branches

In 1991, Frank Bonifay, Jim Ragland, and Kermit Braud, all residents of the hardwood ridge bordering the 17,000-acre Spanish Lake Basin, saved some of the giant, old-growth cypress trees admired by Lousiana's most famous explorer, Iberville, when he arrived here three hundred years ago. Just in time, the three men forged agreements with landowners and parish, state, and federal offices, created the non-profit Bluff Swamp Wildlife Refuge, and bought 901 acres that were scheduled to be clear-cut for their lumber.

Bluff Swamp, now being enhanced and restored, is an ancient wetlands teeming with fish, alligators, wildlife, and resident and migratory birds. Lying on the Mississippi River Flyway, this is a diverse and complex ecosystem, one of few remaining wilderness habitats being restored in the Lower Mississippi River Valley.

Kermit Braud, formerly a county agent with the LSU Cooperative Extension Service, is a gifted Cajun storyteller and historian known for his conservation work. When hunting in the swamp, he and his three brothers still sound the Cajun's bullhorn and stir up a terrific jambalaya over a wood fire. Their family donated their ancestral home to Alligator Bayou Tours, which is restoring it as a living museum and cultural center for children and adults.

Conservationists Frank Bonifay, a visionary of French and Spanish Canary Islander descent, and Jim Ragland, tour guide, wood and glass artist, photographer, and down-home Cajun cook, are co-owners of the popular Alligator Bayou Tours. Cruising passengers into the basin on their tour boat, the Alligator Queen, the business partners educate regional and international visitors on wetlands ecology, wildlife, and the rich history of this area, the cultural cradle of Baton Rouge.

Commemorative plaques mark Alligator Bayou as "one of the prettiest spots" seen by Baton Rouge's French founder, Iberville, on his March 25-29, 1699, journey along the Bayou Manchac shortcut to the Gulf of Mexico. These dates and March 17, 1699, the date that Iberville sighted the red stick, are the basis of Baton Rouge's tricentennial, Bonne Fete, and of FrancoFete, a statewide celebration of three hundred years of French influence in Louisiana.

In 1998, Alligator Bayou Tours and Bluff Swamp Wildlife Refuge won the Louisiana Rural Tourism Success Award for their part in bringing this history to light and for developing a citizen-based public-private partnership that benefits the entire state. All three men are a testament to the persistence and toil that built Louisiana and to the long-term viability of cultural and ecological tourism. These exciting new industries are propelling Louisiana into a more diverse economic future. ⚜

Chapter 4

Food, Festivals, and Music

MmmmMmm. What a menu, cher: turtle soup, shrimp remoulade, crawfish etouffee, crab-stuffed mushrooms, oysters rockefeller, alligator boudin, shrimp and corn soup, pecan pie, and cafe au lait. If that's not tempting enough, how about about a steaming seafood gumbo, crawfish bisque, hot buttered French bread, grilled snapper with crabmeat dressing, spinach madeline, and bread pudding with rum sauce? MmmmMmm.

Louisiana's scrumptious foods, together with music, dancing, and crowds of festive people, are the spice of life for Baton Rougeans. For many people, in fact, they are a tradition and a way of life. In the old days, sharing food helped people survive in the Louisiana wilderness.

Beyond the mere fact of survival, here's how folks began to "pass a good time" in Louisiana centuries ago.

First, a Cajun couple set a big cast iron pot over an open hearth and sauteed diced onions, bell pepper, celery, and garlic in a roux made of lard and flour. A Creole (second generation French or Spanish person born here or a free person of color) poured in a soup stock, called bouillabaisse, flavored with fish or meat. A Choctaw chief tossed in a pinch of filé powder, or ground sassafras leaves. A German woman added sausage, and a Spanish conquistador dropped in a few hot peppers. Africans named the mixture "gombo" for the French Caribbean okra they brought here to thicken the soup. Creoles and Cajuns tossed in hot cayenne peppers and Tabasco sauce sure to bring any pot to a boil!

Fireworks explode above the river at FestForAll and at a patriotic July 4 festival. *Photo by Philip Gould*

Unique and delicious, the rich, dark bouquet of filé gumbo (and, as the song says, jambalaya and crawfish pie-a) still drifts up and away beyond Louisiana to the farthest corners of the world, where millions of people trace these enticing scents back to bayou country, the cradle of cultures which stirred themselves together to create a regional identity unlike any other. Connoisseurs assume, no doubt, that a blend of the world's best foods hints at a story worth telling.

And so it does. Louisiana's spicy, delicious cuisine is the basis of a cultural imperative to *laissez les bon temps roulez*, that is, "let the good times roll" out of the simmering cookpot into music, dancing, festivals, and a *joie de vivre*, or joy of living, that Baton Rougeans are born with. Here, a pot of gumbo, jambalaya, or etouffee calls together a crowd. Soon, a musician pulls out a fiddle or guitar, dancing feet tap the floor, and a party, if not a festival, is brewing.

Baton Rouge, the cultural crossroads of the state, enjoys easy access to upwards of three hundred festivals staged each year in Louisiana towns and cities. Pictured, Henry Gray takes the stage during the annual Baton Rouge Blues Festival. *Photo by Philip Gould*

Baton Rouge, the cultural crossroads of the state, enjoys easy access to upwards of three hundred festivals staged each year in Louisiana

Both Creole and Cajun cuisines relish the shrimp, oysters, crabs, fish, and crawfish for which Louisiana is so well known.
Photos by Philip Gould

towns and cities. Food, music, and dancing, the main events, are often accompanied by zany activities like frog jumping contests, male beauty pageants, pirogue races, hot pepper-eating contests, and, at one ambitious festival, the creation of a culinary masterpiece: a 5,000-egg crawfish omelet cooked for the crowd.

There's no doubt about it: Baton Rougeans revel in the food, festivals, and music that spice up city life—and with good reason: Cajun and Creole cuisines are the most exciting in America today.

John Folse, an internationally acclaimed Louisiana chef, explains the origin of the two French cuisines. Creole food, characterized by flavorful soups and sauces, the use of tomato in tangy sauce piquantes and a rich array of courses, is French aristocratic cooking adapted to the wild game, seafood, vegetables, and spices available in the New Orleans area at the time of Creole settlement in the late 1690s. Since then, Creole cuisine has been influenced by Spanish, German, and Italian cooking.

Cajun cooking, typified by one-pot meals, reflects the way of life in early Louisiana. The exiled French Acadians of Nova Scotia, arriving here in 1755, lived off the land and made their jambalayas, grillades, gumbos, sauce piquantes, and fricassees with fish, shellfish, and wild game snared in bayous, swamps, rivers, and lakes.

Both Creole and Cajun cuisines relish the shrimp, oysters, crabs, fish, and crawfish for which Louisiana is so well known. Bookstores throughout the U.S. and Europe sell cookbooks by chefs and entrepreneurial civic groups sharing their favorite recipes. These tasty dishes are made by fabulous seafood restaurants in the Baton Rouge area. These seafood restaurants and an extraordinary array of excellent ethnic restaurants, explain why Baton Rougeans dine out so often and flock to church fairs and six city festivals.

Festivals spring to life in April with Baton Rouge Earth Day, an eco-celebration that is the largest in the South and recognized as one of the best in America. FestForAll, a weekend-long arts and crafts fest showcasing music, dance and theater on several stages, brings tens of thousands of people to the tree-lined streets of North Boulevard. FestForAll, held in the merry month of May, brings Baton Rougeans downtown to make merry at craft booths, concerts, a Children's Village of hands-on art experiences, dance and poetry tents, and ethnic foods for every taste.

Fireworks explode above the river at FestForAll and at a patriotic July 4 festival sponsored by the U.S.S. Kidd & Nautical Center. Country and 1950s bands perform in late afternoon, followed by marches and military music played by the Baton Rouge Concert Band. At dark, some seventy thousand people gather on the levee for a spectacular fireworks show launched from a barge in the middle of the river.

The cooler winds of September bring superb blues musicians into local schools to teach students about the artform, its birth in Baton Rouge and along the river delta, and how the blues is the basis of almost all popular music. Concerts in different clubs

lead to the rousing Blues Festival on downtown concert stages. Again in October, the oak-shaded downtown boulevard is the setting for the International Heritage Festival. Baton Rouge's fifty ethnic cultures showcase their music, dance, and art to educate, enlighten, and inspire each other.

In late November, gospel music stirs crowds gathered on the levee down by the riverside. Local and regional groups, quartets, and guest soloists sing songs and perform liturgical dance ringing with good gospel news.

Baton Rougeans love parades. Downtown echoes all day with cries of "Throw me somethin', mister!" as thousands of party-goers at the Spanishtown Mardi Gras Parade leap up for colorful beaded necklaces thrown by folks on sixty or more riotous floats. Locals and out-of-towners arrive the day before in campers and RVs to tailgate and barbecue after the parade.

Since the State Capitol looms over this historic neighborhood of artists, professors, and politicians, the parade's hilarious antics always center on government foibles and political misdeeds. It is greatly admired for its cleverness and studied lack of decorum. Poor Taste, in fact, was the theme one year, followed the next by a tongue-in-cheek "Hollywood Comes to Spanish Town" when actor Paul Newman was in town filming "Blaze," a movie about Louisiana's infamous governor Earl K. Long. Baton Rouge has several Mardi Gras krewes, costume balls, and other parades, but this funny, irreverent rolling political commentary is in a category all its own.

Just as zany are the gaily decorated floats in the St. Patrick's Day Parade, which winds its way through an originally Irish neighborhood, Hundred Oaks, and along Perkins Road, an historic business district steeped in personality. Huge crowds gather at parties and festivities on the parade route, whooping it up for the favor of little green trinkets. In December, Christmas parade floats sparkle with white lights and bright red glitter, but the roar of the crowd is still the same: "Throw me somethin', mister."

Christmas on the River, a month-long celebration, is a melange of exciting events, from concerts, plays, ice skating, caroling, and bonfires on the levee to a fireworks display over the river and a spectacular Cajun Christmas

The colorful and flavorful dishes so well associated with Louisiana, such as jambalayas, gumbos, and tangy tomato-based sauce piquantes, have their roots in the Creole and Cajun cultures of early Louisiana settlement.

Photos by Philip Gould

(above) **The holiday season sparkles with festivals of light, music, and family cheer.**
Photo by Philip Gould

(below) In 1999 Baton Rouge celebrated its 300th birthday with Bonne Fete, a year-long series of festivals, special events, and activities for people throughout the area. Bonne Fete was a special part of Louisiana's celebration of 300 years of statehood, "Franco Fete."
Photo by Philip Gould

Wonderland with animated exhibits and 500,000 glittering holiday lights.

Whether it's at cozy jazz clubs, artsy coffee shops, Indian pow-wows, or a zydeco dance in the swamp, Baton Rougeans enjoy gathering to socialize and celebrate—well, anything. Music is usually on tap, and it is especially rich and unique in the capital city, the home of blues, jazz, gospel, Cajun, zydeco, and stylistic hybrids like Louisiana swamp pop.

One of the best places to hear the low-down blues and its rock-influenced offshoot, rhythm & blues, is the rustic Tabby's Blues Box and Heritage Hall. This downtown hotspot is owned by Tabby Thomas, an internationally known recording artist, local radio show host, and dedicated blues conservationist. Listeners from all over the world visit Tabby's to hear legendary blues artists from Baton Rouge, who, like Rockin' Tabby Thomas and His Mighty House Rockers, regularly embark on European concert tours.

Swamp pop, a fusion of Cajun, Creole, and rhythm & blues music, is unique to Louisiana dance halls. South Louisiana is the birthplace of this music, which has exerted an influence on popular music in the U.S. and abroad.

Swamp pop is known for its highly emotional lyrics, honky-tonk piano playing, bellowing saxophones, R&B backbeat, bouncy Cajun rhythms, and black Creole two-steps. It rose out of 1950s and '60s hits like "All These Things" and "I'm Leaving It All Up to You," love songs which made slow-dance and jitterbugging one of life's chief pleasures for many Baton Rougeans. Others step to a different beat, from ballroom to square dancing, folk, Cajun, and zydeco.

Just as Cajun and Creole foods are cultural blends, so are their music and dance. The roots of the two styles reach back to Celtic beginnings that echo faintly in the softer, more traditional Cajun ballads. In Louisiana, French Creole and Acadian music gave a language and lyrics to zydeco, a black Creole musical form enlivened by African rhythms, syncopation, and improvisation. Both types of music flowered in the Louisiana countryside and,

through time, were colored by the Spanish guitar, German accordion, and the wailing, terraced singing style of Louisiana Indians. Anglo-American jigs and reels gave form to Cajun and zydeco tunes, which were fully structured a century ago. Since then, Cajuns added the twin spoons and dried bones as instruments. Zydeco musicians expertly play the metal ridges of the scrubboard.

The steady, measured rhythm and bright, happy character of Cajun music, revived by a 1972 festival, brought the art form out of dance halls onto the concert stage and sparked a cultural renaissance for the people of South Louisiana. The music and the people, as well as their food and dance, are now acclaimed throughout the world, as is zydeco, which has shaken up a worldwide dance craze.

Cajun bands play in rustic bars and at Mulate's and other family restaurants from here to Lafayette. On Friday nights, the Cajun French Music Association (CFMA) hosts a Baton Rouge dance for 350 member families and the public. The CFMA's awe-inspiring exhibition dance troupe, Les Danseurs de la Capitale de Baton Rouge, performs free of charge for area schools, nursing homes, hospitals, festivals, and "wherever there is a need or desire for the Cajun influence," says Gwen Fontenot, the group's coordinator. A children's troupe, Le Joie de Vie, also travels as Cajun

French Creole and Acadian music gave a language and lyrics to zydeco.
Photos by Philip Gould

The cultural diversity of Baton Rouge becomes national unity during the July 4 festival sponsored by the U.S.S. Kidd & Nautical Center, as people of all backgrounds celebrate their common American heritage.
Photo by Philip Gould

ambassadors and, to the delight of audiences, expertly plays the musical spoons.

Alligator Bayou, a cultural landmark, preserves the Cajun and zydeco heritage with seasonal dancing on a bayou-side pavilion in a wetlands basin just below Baton Rouge. Superb zydeco dancers from other cities drive or fly in to Alligator Bayou and rustic clubs in Lafayette's Cajun Country to experience the "roots" of the music. The tireless, perspiring dancers refuel with cold water, spicy gumbo, jambalaya, and new friends, enough to qualify as a festival in themselves.

Music and dancing are two of the nicest things about Baton Rouge. "We don't have kings and queens, princes and princesses," laughs Camille Bercier, a visual artist and marketing consultant, "and we might grow up as poor as a church mouse. But because we have so much joie de vivre, on Friday night you can be king of the dance floor. That's the attitude of people here, and I think it's kind of a unique thing in the United States." ✤

Downtown echoes with cries of "Throw me somethin' mister" as thousands of party-goers at the Spanish Town Mardi Gras parade leap up for colorful beads and trinkets tossed from colorful floats.

Photo by Philip Gould

Chapter 5

Arts Capital

The arts in Baton Rouge weave themselves together like the treasured pieces of a patchwork quilt—warm, lively, and blazing with colors, textures, and patterns that spruce up every season.

On a moonlit summer's eve, the silvery voice of Judy Collins soars with the Baton Rouge Symphony in concert on the lawn of the antebellum-style Hemingbough. At Halloween, LSU professor Don Moore gives a frightfully spooky read to Bram Stoker's "Dracula" on WRKF Public Radio.

The yuletide season springs to life as hundreds of local children leap, dance, and pirouette onstage in Baton Rouge Ballet Theatre's "The Nutcracker," a December family tradition wrapped in sugarplum visions of moss, bayous, and plantation scenery.

And any time of the year, lucky listeners in nightclubs, schools, or churches can hear jazz poet Edith Batiste breathe cosmic truth between silky clarinet notes played by her husband, Alvin Batiste, director of Jazz Studies at Southern University and an internationally known recording artist.

Jane Redding of the Baton Rouge Symphony Chorus stirred audiences during the group's performance of *Messiah*. *Photo by Philip Gould*

The St. Francis Xavier Sacred Dancers performed for a Martin Luther King Day celebration. *Photo by Philip Gould*

In Baton Rouge, the arts are more than entertainment; they weave in and out of people's lives, lift up hearts and minds, and draw them together in a single fabric: an arts quilt by far greater than the sum of its pieces. And yet, the wholeness of the quilt can only be seen in separate pieces, each of which tell a story:

On weekend nights, Tabby's Blues Box and Neal's Restaurant howl as blues greats Tabby Thomas, Henry Gray, Raful Neal and his son, Kenny Neal—international performers and recording artists—jam together and fire up the stage. Blues lovers visiting from all over the world hang on every soulful bended note.

On a Sunday afternoon at De La Ronde Hall, the Louisiana Sinfonietta premieres a world class concerto by its Greek-born founder and conductor, Dinos Constantinides, an LSU professor and composer with major works on sixteen CDs. On other days, the Sinfonietta shares the beauty of its music: a violinist gives a talk at a library; a cellist performs in a nursing home.

At Baton Rouge Little Theater, a New York choreographer, courtesy of an Arts Council grant, works with local dancers performing in the musical comedy, "Gypsy." It is a smash hit, with audiences laughing uproariously at the antics of Gypsy Rose Lee's pushy mother. During the three-week run, the choreographer presents half a dozen workshops to theater students and professionals.

The atmosphere crackles in the Catfish Town Atrium at a sophisticated multimedia art show, a Summer Sizzler put on by Baton Rouge Gallery, complete with delicious hors d'oeuvres and swing dancing to the Buddy Lee Orchestra. At LSU's annual Festival of Contemporary Music, In the Company of Dancers whips into high-voltage choreography set to computer-generated music.

Anna Williams has won widespread acclaim for her intricate work in the art of quilting. *Photo by Philip Gould*

People watching Swine Palace's modern-day production of "The Merchant of Venice" are held spellbound by the brilliance of Shakespeare as portrayed by Louisiana actors and their British director, Barry Kyle.

As always, art is a sensory experience in the patterns of life—color, tone, shape, form, and texture held in harmony and balance. That is precisely the lesson taught by a Chinese artist visiting LSU as part of a cultural exchange. An Arts Council grant enables him to teach middle school artists how to paint on rice paper, from the heart.

It would take a massive quilt, indeed, to portray the arts in Baton Rouge, which, for a medium-sized city, is nevertheless an artistic mecca. Perhaps the river's energy generates the wellspring of talent pouring out of blues and jazz musicians, primitive painters, quilters, basketweavers, gospel singers, and liturgical dancers. Whatever the source, one thing is certain: the richness of the arts in Baton Rouge flows out of the city's cultural diversity.

Without a doubt, art unites people. It's a common language, a song dissolving barriers in gender, race, and religion. The arts enlighten us, and in the face of understanding, cultural differences fall away. Audiences nod in agreement: "Yeah, that was a cool sax riff." "Wow, can they dance!" "Ahhh, now I see... now I understand," we say.

The beauty of Baton Rouge's arts quilt is its being stitched together, as at a quilting bee, by many thousands of art lovers. These community volunteers, closely focused on the task at hand, grasp the intrinsic function of the arts: to deepen knowledge, raise consciousness, build character, and spark creativity by challenging old ways of seeing things.

Baton Rougeans are keenly aware of other

advantages, as well: the arts as a powerful economic development tool—a red brush, if you will, used to "paint the town rouge" with life and prosperity. By attracting tourists, residents, and new business to the city, the arts pay high dividends in economic development. Today, with investment on the rise, Baton Rouge is amassing arts capital and becoming an arts capital.

Since the early 1990s, the Arts Council of Greater Baton Rouge has taken a lead role in a community-wide partnership that is revitalizing downtown and expanding the city's horizons. Create Baton Rouge, a cultural plan for the millennium, arose out of a 1992 city planning process and by 1996 took shape through steering committees, task forces, surveys, assessments, and town meetings.

The goals of Create Baton Rouge are to strengthen arts education in schools and communities, develop neighborhood programs to provide access to the arts, connect the community through a downtown arts district, and expand economic opportunities for artists and arts businesses. Driving the project is the gaiety of a city investing its heart in the arts and, as a byproduct, getting a facelift.

Along Third Street, downtown's main thoroughfare, the display windows of empty buildings sparkle with exhibits of stained glass, sculptures, paintings, handmade jewelry, photographs, fabric art, and much more. The temporary exhibits, called Phantom Galleries, spruce up downtown, showcase work by student and professional artists, and draw attention to buildings for lease or sale. International themes by exhibitors like the Chinese Culture Club and the Arts India Council inform passersby about the city's rich cultural resources.

Today, the Arts District is a festive sight, with colorful banners and gala building murals beckoning visitors to phantom galleries, artist studios, galleries, art exhibits in coffee shops and businesses, and a high-quality Arts Market on Saturdays.

While art and artists redesign downtown, Create Baton Rouge animates other parts of the city. The Zion City CommUNITY Arts Corps staged a "Lifting Hearts Through Art" program on non-violence and inspired a Baptist church to open the Faith Chapel Academy of the Visual and Performing Arts. Encouraged by these successes, civic and church groups wrote grants for programs to help address social problems and urban blight through the arts.

The East Baton Rouge Parish School Board has included the arts in a long-term effort to upgrade school facilities. Blueprints for new buildings call for work spaces and stages for the visual and performing arts. During the evening and in summertime, these art spaces will beckon community classes and programs.

Baton Rouge's arts renaissance is fueled by a powerful synergy, a partnership among most of the powers that be: city-parish government, the Downtown Development District, the Baton Rouge Area Foundation, the Baton Rouge Area Convention & Visitors Bureau, Baton Rouge Recreation and Park Commission, East Baton Rouge Parish School System and Volunteer Baton Rouge. Projecting a $3.1 million community investment over five years, the partnership also includes fifty community groups, hundreds of committed volunteers, and staff members based at the Arts Council.

Create Baton Rouge is sculpted out of a legacy of grassroots involvement in the arts. In the 1970s, preservationist Sue Turner and the late Adalie Brent, a painter and stained glass artist, worked with then-Mayor W.W. Dumas to convert an old city railroad depot into a riverfront art museum. Brent and Turner flew to Notre Dame University to meet the family of a Rodin

Baton Rouge is home to Paul Dufour, the "father of glass art in the Southern United States." His work may be seen in churches and the Catholic Life Center.
Photo by Philip Gould

contemporary, the twentieth-century sculptor, Ivan Mestrovic, a Yugoslav exile whose wartime escape from Hitler and Mussolini was orchestrated by the Vatican. Mestrovic's widow and his daughter, Maria, befriended the Baton Rouge women and sold or loaned the museum the second largest collection of Mestrovic sculptures in the Western hemisphere.

Today, the Louisiana Arts and Science Center (LASC) hosts traveling national exhibits and is a regional catalyst for arts and science education. Students of all ages take field trips to LASC to experience the Mestrovic sculptures, Egyptian mummies, the elements of art in Discovery Depot, and hands-on science in Science Station and the Challenger Learning Center. Some sixty thousand people currently visit LASC each year, but that number is expected to double or triple with its new planetarium and space theater, a $6.8 million project funded by city and state grants. The only one of its kind in America, LASC's tilted, 60-foot-wide cyberdome is designed with inclined stadium seating for viewing sky shows and large-format adventure films like IMAX.

Also in the 1970s, community volunteers established the Arts and Humanities Council of Greater Baton Rouge, which organized four annual festivals and a city-funded grants program. A decade later, the agency handed over its festivals to the city, created a united fund drive and focused on arts education and grant programs.

The Louisiana Arts and Science Center houses the second largest collection of Ivan Mestrovic sculptures in the Western hemisphere.
Photo by Philip Gould

The Baton Rouge arts community has grown geometrically since then, with at least 150 artists supporting themselves through local sale of their works. A fluent, dynamic exchange of ideas, energized by the two universities, is strong enough to attract artists here from world capitals. In turn, these maestros guide local artists to success in Baton Rouge and beyond.

If, indeed, the best measure of a city is its art, then a glance at key players on the arts stage should reveal a story.

The Baton Rouge Symphony Orchestra, fifty years old in 1998-99, is a professional community orchestra and one of few in the nation consistently operating in the black. Accessible yet challenging music and affordable ticket prices sell out classical and pops concerts, family matinees, an outdoor concert series, and holiday extravaganzas. In the 1980s, Conductor Emeritus James Paul, a recipient of the coveted Leonard Bernstein American Conductor's Appointment, ushered the Baton Rouge Symphony to a critically acclaimed performance in Carnegie Hall.

Baton Rouge is a city of music, with choirs, choruses, barbershop quartets, the Gilbert & Sullivan Society, the Sweet Adelines, gospel groups and remarkably talented soloists performing in churches and concert halls. The city turns out for red-hot original musicals by the Baton Rouge Community Chorus & Playhouse and for concerts by Louisiana's Absolute Pitch. This choral group of fifty African-American children recently toured France and was visited in return by the French Chorale and the Boys Choir of Quebec.

Each year, the universities host two international music events. Southern University's three-day Tourgee DeBose National Piano Competition brings students and professional pianists here to vie for awards and scholarships. LSU's two-week Festival of Contemporary

Music premieres works by leading conductors and composers. Both events feature workshops and clinics.

Six companies offer theater lovers a variety of choices. Children thrill to the original and classical works performed by Playmakers, Louisiana's only professional theater company for young audiences and one of only a handful in the South. Adult audiences delight in the comedies, whodunits and Broadway musicals presented by Baton Rouge Little Theater and Baker Little Theater. Classical and contemporary plays are the emphasis of drama departments at Southern University and LSU.

Baton Rougeans are especially proud of Swine Palace Productions, a world class repertory company adding innovative twists and sometimes regional flair to celebrated works of Southern literature and to the classics. Director Barry Kyle left the Royal Shakespeare Company in London and Stratford to establish this professional theater. Named for its newly renovated home in a former agricultural exhibit hall at LSU, Swine Palace is an artistic trailblazer showcasing Louisiana art and artists in a cathedral-like theater with cutting-edge light and sound systems.

Literature is in full bloom here, with published poets, novelists, and playwrights reading their works in galleries, college auditoriums, and at festivals. One catalyst is the highly respected creative writing department at LSU and the English department's legacy of famous writers beginning with poet Robert Penn Warren, winner of a Pulitzer Prize for "All the King's Men" and co-founder of LSU's respected literary periodical, "The Southern Review."

Readers and Writers, an affiliate of LSU's English department, presents a literary season showcasing local and national talent, while the department itself sponsors a nationally recognized annual poetry festival, "A Gathering of Poets." The rest of the year, writers meet in libraries and coffee shops to talk craft and get critiques on their current work.

In its heyday, Tabby's Blues Box hosted jam sessions featuring such notable performers as Tabby Thomas (the club's namesake, pictured below), Henry Gray, Raful Neal, and his son Kenny Neal.
Photos c.1985 by Philip Gould

The yuletide season springs to life with the Baton Rouge Ballet Theatre's annual performance of "The Nutcracker," a December family tradition.
Photo by Philip Gould

Baton Rouge has a lively community of visual artists, a number of whom have gained regional, national, and even international fame. Works by Paul Dufour, the father of glass art in the Southern United States, may be seen in churches and the Catholic Life Center. Sculptures by the late Frank Hayden, a student of Ivan Mestrovic, grace the downtown area and a museum on the campus of Southern University.

The Southern and LSU art faculties set high standards for visual art and exhibit their own work in competitions and shows at the universities, public schools, the Louisiana Art and Artists' Guild, Baton Rouge Gallery, and the Louisiana Arts and Science Center. Photographers like LSU's A.J. Meek and the late Fonville Winans and Alban E. Woolley have established photography as an art form. Two hundred photos by Woolley, a gypsy photojournalist and author of twenty books, chronicle the 1940s to 1960s and may be seen in the Louisiana and Lower Mississippi Valley Collections at LSU's Hill Memorial Library. Woolley depicted extraordinary people in exotic settings and at pivotal moments in world history.

Some of the city's finest talent has been nourished by Arts Council grants to artists and performing arts organizations. The Multicultural Arts Grants Program, for example, serves to acquaint the community with gifted artists and brings them the honor they deserve. Recent grant recipients include bluesman Tabby Thomas and art quilter Anna Williams.

A few years ago, the state of Louisiana demonstrated a long-term commitment to the arts by voting into law the Decentralized Arts Funding Program, a 50-cent per capita assessment statewide supporting everything from inner-city schools and churches to youth organizations and arts groups. The Arts Council of Greater Baton Rouge administers this program for an 11-parish region.

City-parish government dedicates upwards of $50,000 annually to grant programs designed to increase the regional quality of life, while Baton Rouge businesses support the arts through the Community Fund for the Arts Campaign. This united arts drive, operated by the Arts Council, allocates operating funds to fourteen established arts organizations with budgets amounting to $10.1 million. CFA recipients range from the Baton Rouge Area Convention & Visitors Bureau, which stages FestForAll, an annual arts and crafts festival, to the Baton Rouge Symphony and WRKF Public Radio. In 1998, 887 companies contributed more than $700,000 to the fund drive. More than thirty companies participate in a workplace giving program involving thousands of employees.

As a cultural catalyst, the Arts Council works to enhance basic education and to inspire young artists and art lovers in the schools, thereby sowing a new crop of talent and audiences for those artists. Education programs range from three-unit lessons on a single discipline to five-week and nine-week residencies in which teams of artists integrate their disciplines into the school's core curriculum.

CFA funds allocated to Playmakers help support the writing of educational productions by local playwrights (fun examples include "The Phenomenal Anatomical Adventure" and "The Mathmagical Journey") presented in spring tours of parish elementary schools. In summer, original plays touring more than fifty libraries encourage kids to read.

In an Arts Meets Science program, local musicians like jazz pianist Maynard Batiste improvise songs to animate the "natures" of swamp animals. Actors teach kids role playing and, in the process, sharpen their problem-solving skills. Each one of these programs enhances basic learning, broadens intellectual horizons and taps into creative talents children might not discover otherwise.

Unlike anything else, the arts enrich Baton Rougeans while neatly paying for themselves. In 1998, the arts had a $40 million economic impact on the city, with audience dollars multiplying into revenues for local restaurants, hotels, parking lots, transportation companies, and retail businesses. Each dollar stimulates a program or performance and spins off again and again into the economies of the metro area. Statistics say that each dollar spent on an arts performance generates another $5 to $10.

The arts: a work in progress. Baton Rouge will be a pleasure to observe in decades to come, as artists and economists shape and reshape the city's future. By capitalizing on the arts, Baton Rouge will steadily raise its quality of life while satisfying the human hunger to create and to enjoy what is created. ⚜

Art can be found in the very buildings of Baton Rouge, perhaps best exemplified by the intricate carvings and statues that decorate the State Capitol, which tell the story of the city and state.

Photo by Philip Gould

TIGERS

Chapter 6

Things to Do, Places to Be

When brisk weather is in the air, it's football season in Baton Rouge and time for tailgate parties, banner waving, football cards, and, in general, the high-spirited hijinks so common to South Louisiana. On game nights, LSU turns purple and gold with balloons, streamers, pom-poms, and excited fans dressed in glitzy purple and gold clothing. The owner of a car dealership parades a purple and gold Cadillac to the game, and a private pilot dips the wings of his purple and gold plane over the field. In the eyes of a zany ophthalmologist sparkle one purple and one gold contact lens.

The fun starts the night before each game, when motor homes and camper trucks pull into LSU parking lots for two days of partying. Families bring barbecue pits, jambalaya cookpots, kegs of beer, and all manner of food, drink and entertainment, gathering to cheer on good times and the Fighting Tigers.

Southern University's tailgate parties are a jamboree, too, yet only a taste of the revelry in a halftime performance by Southern's sensational marching band. The tall, gangly drum major, wearing a military blue coat and gold pants, runs onto the playing field in a high, knee-lift strut to a drumroll, faces the band and bends backward until his head touches the field.

Fall means football in Baton Rouge, bringing tailgate parties, banner waving, and high-spirited hijinks for fans of the state's two major universities—Louisiana State University and Southern University—as well as local youth, junior high, and high school action.
Photo by Philip Gould

The crowd goes wild at this "limbo" ritual, and the band strikes up a hip-hop tune, the "Star Wars" theme, a fast march, or a Michael Jackson moonwalk. Dancers tumble onto the field. The show is on. The 170-piece Jaguar Marching Band, voted number one in the nation by *U.S.A. Today*, stars at Sugar Bowl and Super Bowl games, televised pro games, and has appeared in NFL film specials and at three presidential inaugurations.

Southern and LSU games, after all of this buildup, are frenzied competitions and, win or lose, as much the talk of the town as Louisiana politics. On game nights, with traffic jamming up the two universities and all roads leading to and from, life is pretty much on hold. A good bet is to reach that movie, dance hall, or coffee shop early but, even there, know that devotees with radios may shout out the game scores.

It's all in good fun and a taste of the competitive spirit that buoys the city when the Baton Rouge Kingfish, a professional franchise team of the East Coast Hockey League, or the Bayou Beast, a professional indoor football team, play at the Riverside Centroplex.

The Baton Rouge Sports Foundation, by attracting national champsionship games and sports leagues like the Kingfish, capitalizes on the city's love affair with sports and recreation. In 1996, the Olympic Torch lit a cauldron fire

The State Capitol's 27th-floor observation deck is a favorite stopping place for the building's visitors, affording a bird's eye view of the river, the city, and points beyond. *Photo by Philip Gould*

Just below Baton Rouge are several impressive antebellum mansions, including Houmas House on the river's east bank.
Photo by Philip Gould

eight thousand children and teens playing in leagues operated by the Baton Rouge Soccer Association, play tournaments at schools and in parks.

If you ask Baton Rougeans what they love best about the city, most will cite the friendly people, terrific food, and long growing season. With eight to ten months of warm, sunny weather, people enjoy the outdoors almost year-round. This is reflected in the city's rich recreational opportunities.

In 1946, the Baton Rouge Recreation & Park Commission (BREC) was established as a political subdivision of the state with an operating budget of $10,000. Parish residents are consistently delighted to pay for park pleasures: By 1960, that budget jumped to $710,000 and, by 1996, to $18 million.

downtown for thirty-five thousand spectators. The same year, the city hosted an Olympic baseball exhibition game between America and Australia, courtesy of Skip Bertman, five-time National Coach of the Year and head coach of the U.S. Olympic Baseball Team and the LSU baseball team, which won two straight national titles for a total of four this decade.

In recent years, Baton Rouge has been a hotbed of sporting events, including the Women's International Bowling Congress, the U.S. National Hot Air Balloon Championship, the International Special Olympics, Senior Olympics, and the U.S.A. Track & Field Junior Olympics, which is the world's largest track meet. Recently, Baton Rouge became the national headquarters of the National Senior Games Association. City government and volunteers with the Baton Rouge Sports Foundation work actively to capture these honors, which reap considerable economic benefits.

During the rest of the year, adult and intercollegiate soccer teams, plus

BREC operates a unique array of programs, facilities, and services, most notably the Greater Baton Rouge Zoo, Magnolia Mound Plantation, the L.H. Cohn Arboretum, the Independence Park Botanic Garden, Bluebonnet Swamp Nature Center, and the Highland Road Astronomical Observatory. The department also provides facility space for Baton Rouge Gallery and studio and exhibition space for the Louisiana Art and Artists' Guild Gallery.

As for sports, there are opportunities from A to Z: airgun and archery ranges, a BMX raceway, campgrounds, two disc golf courses and regular tournaments, an equestrian arena with

The Blue Bayou Water Park is a refreshing way to beat the heat of a Baton Rouge summer. *Photo by Philip Gould*

Many people relax and stay fit by walking, jogging, or riding bikes around the City Park Lakes and University Lakes near LSU. *Photo by Philip Gould*

riding lessons and children's day camps, fishing lakes, fitness centers, six golf courses, indoor tracks, in-line rollerblading, mountain bike trails and a race series, fifty-one recreation centers, sports leagues, tennis tournaments, unicycle classes, velodrome cycling and zoo programs for kids and teens. Sports teams include basketball, softball, tee-ball and flag and tackle football.

The 176 parks owned by BREC operate a full events schedule. In addition to daily sports practice, team and tournament playoffs, and use by community groups, city parks are home to arts and cultural activities and entertainment. Preschoolers celebrate art, singing, and basic learning at morning playgroups, while Playmakers teaches creative drama and play production almost year-round. Older citizens enjoy tea dances, shuffleboard, ping-pong, soccer, hay rides, and cook-outs at nearly two dozen centers. People of all ages attend the parties and parades sponsored by BREC at Mardi Gras, Easter, and Christmas.

BREC's Greater Baton Rouge Zoo is a busy source of family entertainment. For years, "Buckskin Bill" Black, school board member and former host of a children's TV program, ended his shows with the catchphrase, "Baton Rouge needs a zoo." Listeners collected 600,000 pennies to buy the first animal, but it was enough to purchase two elephants, Penny One and Penny Two, who brought about the zoo's opening in 1970. Today, the Greater Baton Rouge Zoo is a premier zoological park with a focus on natural ecosystems. Amphitheater shows, student workshops, an outreach zoomobile, and annual celebrations like Zippety Zoo Day and Zoobilations make this a rich source of education and entertainment in Baton Rouge.

Magnolia Mound Plantation, a 1791 French Creole plantation, gives tours in period costumes and offers creative children's programs like Grandmother's Trunk and A Step Back in Time. Open hearth cooking in the fall and several festivals, including a Civil War reenactment, make this a valuable city attraction. While the home, its kitchen garden and crop garden evoke the lives of aristocratic Creoles, an 1830s slave cabin recalls the story beyond the "big house."

Magnolia Mound, saved in the 1960s by the Foundation for Historical Louisiana, is one of the finest restorations on the Great River Road. Its wide galleries, French doors, and Caribbean details distinguish it architecturally from the stately, columned mansions of the Old South.

A Sunday drive along levee back roads is a scenic journey into history. The winding River Road, to the south of Baton Rouge, leads to the "great houses" of the vast sugar plantations farmed in the wetlands of South Louisiana. Highway 61 north leads to the hilly high ground of the great cotton plantations.

Most of these houses, especially Laura Plantation, the Creole home of the Br'er Rabbit tales, recount vivid personal stories that make their tours memorable. Sprawling, moss-draped oak trees shade all of them and were often planted in a magnificent alley meant to funnel breezes from the river to the home.

Just below Baton Rouge are several impressive antebellum mansions, notably the historic Houmas House on the river's east bank and on the west bank, the stunning Nottoway, said to be the largest plantation home in the South.

In English-dominated St. Francisville, a 30-minute drive north of Baton Rouge, more than 140 structures in the historic district are listed

The Greater Baton Rouge Zoo is a premier zoological park with a focus on natural ecosystems. *Photo by Philip Gould* on the National Register of Historic Places. Just beyond the town are seven historic homes, including Oakley Plantation,where John James Audubon, the famous naturalist, lived while painting eighty of the works in his "Birds of America" series. Oakley is part of a 100-acre state park.

Across the river in French-settled New Roads is Parlange Plantation, home to the charming "Miss Lucy," who enjoys serving sherry to visitors while regaling them with stories of her Creole ancestors. In the friendly city of New Roads, excellent Cajun and Creole food is served at restaurants overlooking False River, once a bend in the Mississippi River and now an oxbow lake used for fishing and boating.

The fabled French Louisiana country of bayous, marshes, rivers, and lakes offers beautiful woods and waters for fishing, hunting, boating, skiing, and nature photography. A common sight on Louisiana highways is a vehicle pulling a boat to False River, the Amite, Blood and Blind, the Tchefuncte, and many others. People of all ages enjoy settling themselves and a drink-filled ice chest into large inner tubes and floating down the Tangipahoa and other long, winding rivers not too far away.

Aside from country jaunts, the best way to learn about Louisiana is to spend time at the Rural Life Museum and Windrush Gardens in Baton Rouge. A self-guided walking tour leads into a complex of furnished buildings such as those found on a working plantation: a commissary, blacksmith's shop, sugarhouse, grist mill, overseer's house, school house, and more. In a separate complex, examples of folk architecture include shotgun, dogtrot and Acadian homes. The museum, an LSU department with a library, also includes the 25-acre Windrush Gardens, an expanse of formal gardens with statuary, winding paths, lakes, and plants indigenous to nineteenth century Louisiana. The West Baton Rouge Museum, located across the river in Port Allen, contains a sugar mill and other interesting historical exhibits.

Some would say that Louisiana politics is the most amusing entertainment in Baton Rouge, and it's true that since the 1920s, more and better quips, jokes, filibusters, threats, and promises have been heard here than anywhere else. Today's political orators, albeit more restrained than in the past, may be heard in the spectator galleries of the House and Senate in the State Capitol (and also in the building's bathrooms, via intercom).

The Art Deco building is a must-see. Completed in 1932 at the height of the Great Depression, it is still the tallest state capitol in America. Its entrance stairs chronicle U.S. history by devoting one step to each state, in the order of their admission. (Alaska and Hawaii belatedly share the top step.) Monumental statues of The Patriots and The Pioneers flank the stairs, while allegorical winged figures guard a twenty-second floor cutaway of the tower in a memorial to Law, Science, Philosophy, and Art.

Superior workmanship abounds in paintings and sculptures seen throughout the building. In the basement is a Louisiana folklife exhibit of handcrafted items such as sunbonnets, quilts, a Mardi Gras costume, and a wooden pirogue. The State Capitol's twenty-seventh-floor observation deck affords a bird's-eye view of the river, the city, and points beyond.

The legends of Louisiana politics come to life at the Center for Political and Governmental History in the Old State Capitol. It is the state repository of film footage from a vintage collection and from television stations in New Orleans and Baton Rouge. A multimedia exhibit features, among other high points, film clips of the late Gov. Huey Long caroling his famous composition, "Every Man A King," and former Gov. Jimmie Davis playing his guitar and belting out his famous song, "You Are My Sunshine." The center also interviews contemporary politicians as part of an ongoing oral history video program. Scholars and other interested parties may request access to a film and video library on Earl and Huey Long.

The Old State Capitol possesses its own unique history, as well. The beautiful, neo-

The State Capitol, completed in 1932, is the tallest state capitol in America. Its entrance steps chronicle U.S. history by devoting one step to each state, in the order of their admission. The Capitol also features intricate statues and carvings, and houses the Louisiana Folklife Exhibit.
Photo by Philip Gould

Gothic statehouse was the site of the infamous impeachment proceedings against then-Gov. Huey Long and is today thought to have a ghost, Pierre, who bangs doors, rumples an antique bed on exhibit, and switches on lights in the middle of the night.

A walk along the riverfront plaza leads to one of the most interesting military exhibits in America, the U.S.S. Kidd & Nautical Center. The Kidd, a World War II Fletcher class destroyer, was saved from a scrap yard in 1982 and towed to Baton Rouge, where volunteers spent countless hours restoring the ship. Home to everything from military reunions to children's slumber parties, the Kidd is an integral part of the city. Its memorial foundation stages an annual 4th of July Festival, and the Kidd's guns fire in honor of every major event in Baton Rouge. The Nautical Center features a P-40 fighter plane, an A-7E Corsair attack aircraft, the largest model ship collection in the South, an eternal flame at the Louisiana Memorial Plaza, and other exhibits paying tribute to war veterans.

Next door to the Nautical Center is the historic Catfish Town, named for the catfish washed up and left flopping by river tides in the days before the levee. Today, Catfish Town, owned by Argosy Gaming, serves up catfish and other Louisiana foods at several restaurants, three of them in a dazzling glass atrium with a stage for festivals and community events. A raised brick-and-glass walkway leads from the atrium to a casino riverboat, The Belle of Baton Rouge, which brings in local and national popular bands.

Upriver is another gambling boat, Casino Rouge, which also keeps the concert scene exciting. Both riverboats sail the muddy Mississippi every few hours.

Visitors enjoy the river view along Red Stick Plaza, with its commemorative sculptures, fountains, and lamplit benches. A raised walkway and staircase leads to the Louisiana Arts

The U.S.S. Kidd & Nautical Center offers a glimpse into the military history of Baton Rouge. The complex also is home to the Louisiana Memorial Plaza, which is the site of an eternal flame that pays tribute to war veterans.

Photos by Philip Gould

(above) Lush swamps, winding bayous, wide vistas of Louisiana birds, and a remarkably rich cultural history attract visitors to the Spanish Lake Basin and the Bluebonnet Swamp Nature Center. *Photo by Philip Gould*

(opposite page) Louisiana Governor Mike Foster took to the highway on a Harley as he led a motorcycle rally from the State Capitol steps to benefit the United Way. *Photo by Philip Gould*

and Science Center, home to traveling exhibits, Discovery Depot for children and The Challenger Center, a high-tech rocket simulator used by children and adults. Across the street, and adjacent to a series of cascading fountains, is the Riverside Centroplex, with its entertainment arena, a 2,000-seat Theatre of the Performing Arts, and the city-parish Governmental Building. In open areas around the Centroplex are works by the world-renowned twentieth century sculptor, Ivan Mestrovic, and his student, the late Frank Hayden, who was a professor at Southern University. On loan to the Louisiana Arts and Science Center is the second largest collection of Mestrovic sculptures in the Western hemisphere.

Day or night, it is a pleasure to walk along the riverfront and through the historic downtown. Dozens of landmarks, homes, buildings, and churches listed on the National Register of Historic Places are described in a self-guided tour pamphlet available from the Foundation for Historical Louisiana. Housed in the newly renovated Old Governor's Mansion, this non-profit group works to preserve the state's cultural and architectural heritage. The Foundation also operates a gift shop and historical museum in the Pentagon Barracks and the State Capitol's Shop at the Top, which sells Louisiana heritage items and souvenirs.

At the end of the day and on weekends, many people relax by walking, jogging, or riding bikes around the City Park Lakes and University Lakes near LSU. Encircled by giant live oaks, the lakes and their neighborhoods are picturesque and refreshing year-round.

To commune more deeply with nature, ride out to the BREC Bluebonnet Swamp Nature Center just south of LSU. Wander along two miles of walkways in a rich, green cypress-tupelo swamp and watch for turtles, alligators, and other wetland species. This natural history park, depicting the interrelationships between man and nature, features a large interpretive center, nature programs, naturalist-guided tours, and a monthly birding walk. Some sixty-five of its 101 acres were donated to BREC by the Louisiana Nature Conservancy.

Lush swamps, winding bayous, wide vistas of Louisiana birds, and a remarkably rich cultural history attract visitors to the 17,000-acre Spanish Lake Basin below the city's southern ridges. Canoeists, boaters, fishermen, and tourists cruising aboard the "Alligator Queen," a 49-passenger tour barge, enjoy the spectacular sunsets behind Cypress Flats, an open lake teeming with resident birds and migratory species winging along the Mississippi River Flyway. With its alligators, ducks, egrets, herons, ibises, bald eagles, and ancient, old-growth cypress trees, the Spanish Lake Basin is a hidden jewel protected by area conservationists. Locals and international visitors go there to enjoy the beauty and serenity of the landscape.

To be, to do or to "doobie-doobie-do" ... that is the jazzy question. Cheer for your favorite team, walk among whispering oaks, or take to the highway for a Cajun *fais-do-do*. In Baton Rouge, there is a season—and some good, spicy seasoning—for any kind of celebration.

Chapter 7

Easy Living in the Friendly City

In early March, Baton Rouge bursts into color with the blooming of redbud trees, dogwoods; masses of pink, purple, and white azaleas, and an artist's palette of new, filmy greens. It is a sight for sore wintry eyes and the debut of a grand flowering that deepens and lasts for the rest of the year.

City neighborhoods are lively gardens fed by bountiful sunshine and rain. People take pleasure in beautifying their homes with native plants like sweet olive, mock orange, gardenias, camellias, Louisiana iris, and Southern magnolia, the state tree. Neighborhoods blossom into their own unique personalities, each shaded by lovely canopies of green that once named this the City of Trees.

The oldest neighborhoods, featuring homes on the National Register of Historic Places, overflow with interesting stories. Spanish Town was developed in 1805 as a refuge for Canary Islander families settled at Bayou Manchac and the Amite River. The military farmers suffered nearly three decades of hurricanes, floods, and epidemics before the Spanish government agreed to move them to this high ground in downtown Baton Rouge, a stone's throw from the riverfront.

History lives in the stately plantation homes in and around Baton Rouge, as reflected in the stately architecture of the Oak Alley Plantation.
Photo by Philip Gould

> "Our homes, buildings, and landmarks on the National Register are vestiges of a remarkable and unique heritage. The architectural detailing is beautiful and inspires us to remember that what we're doing in the present will one day be in the past. We want those following in our footsteps to be proud of what we did."
>
> **Carolyn Bennett,**
> **executive director, Foundation for Historical Louisiana**

Walking through Spanish Town is a delight. It is a hodgepodge of architectural styles dating back to 1823, with stately antebellum homes, mostly Classical Revival, rubbing elbows with charming cottages, Louisiana's long, narrow shotgun houses, and Craftsman-style bungalows on short, tree-lined streets. On windy days, the happy music of riverboat calliopes mingles with wedding bells pealing from landmark churches in the neighborhood. The State Capitol towers overhead.

City history is quite literally built into Spanish Town. Two fine old homes were made of 1830s ship timbers, and another bears pelican door knobs and door plates left over from construction of the State Capitol in the early 1930s. A night watchman employed there purloined the treasures and, later, a hood ornament from Huey Long's Cadillac -- a leaping fish crowned to symbolize the self-styled Kingfish.

Several years ago, "Unsolved Mysteries" filmed a segment in Spanish Town about Long's assassination by Dr. Carl Weiss, who was so well-loved, especially by neighborhood children, that few believe him to have been capable of hurting anyone.

Another celebrated resident was Castro Carrazo, a noted musician brought here to serve as LSU's band director. Long spent a great deal of time at Carrazo's piano, which produced the famous campaign song, "Every Man A King." Carrazo's bungalow is today used for music events in Spanish Town, home to the jazzy, irreverent Spanish Town Mardi Gras Parade. Since the turn of the century, Spanish Town has been the eclectic home of students, professors, artists, politicians, lobbyists, and regal ladies in their nineties.

In contrast, the 1806 Beauregard Town, located only a few blocks away, was a grand, fashionable neighborhood in its time. Today it

Beauregard Town was a grand, fashionable neighborhood of the early 1800s, and today is a favorite with young professionals and "urban pioneers" who are restoring the historic homes.
Photo by Philip Gould

is home to a mix of downtown workers, college professors, lawyers, and urban pioneers who have restored many historic homes. The Old State Capitol, the old courthouse, and the new governmental complex are considered part to this downtown neighborhood.

Captain Elias Beauregard, a New Orleans-born Frenchman and Spanish commandante, laid out a neighborhood plan in the manner of grand European cities: four diagonal streets radiated from a public square surrounded by plazas, gardens, a convent, cathedral, coliseum, and cemetery. The neighborhood, spanning eight square blocks, reached its heyday after the Civil War. Its noteworthy homes include 1900s mansions on North Boulevard, estate-sized houses, a 150-year-old Acadian cottage, bungalows, shotgun, and double shotgun homes.

Like Spanish Town, this shady, charming neighborhood, rich with fine architectural details, is fondly held in memory by old Baton Rouge families whose parents and grandparents grew up there.

In the early 1900s, Baton Rougeans could pay a nickel to "ride the belt" all day. At the eastern edge of the streetcar's loop was the city's first restricted subdivision. It was located a walloping ten blocks from downtown, so the realty company sold its first lots for $150 each.

Despite the distance from downtown, this elegant, fashionable subdivision built up quickly, hastened by a publicity contest to name it. A local woman won a $5 gold piece for the winning entry: Roseland Terrace, a tribute to the white Cherokee roses that climbed on a fence around the city's old racetrack, the site of the subdivision. Many of its streets—Tulip, Olive, Wisteria, Oleander, and Cherokee—commemorate the roses on the Magnolia Race Track.

Roseland Terrace hit a peak of popularity in the 1920s, when City Park was built nearby. The park had a pool, golf course, zoo, carousel, and lakes for fishing or rowing. Wealthy residents built grand estates next to bungalows, double shotguns, and attractive cottages.

Through the years, young live oak trees grew tall enough to spread their green canopies over these well-kept historic homes. Today, three small neighborhoods—Roseland Terrace, Drehr Place, and Kleinert Terrace—compose the Garden District, a lovely, charming community well deserving of its name and listings on the National Register.

In the mid-1930s, citizens moved still farther from downtown into three landmark neighborhoods, College Town, University Gardens, and Southdowns. These areas are still highly desirable for their eclectic architectural mix, the proximity of the City Park Lakes and LSU campus, and the lovely, sprawling old oak trees that shade these neighborhoods.

Winding along the City Park Lakes and University Lakes are magnificent, showpiece homes ranking as some of the most expensive in the city. LSU Avenue, south of campus, merits similar praise. Farther south, several rambling, tree-shaded neighborhoods, like University Hills and University Acres, offer some of the most attractive, well-designed, and affordable homes in the city. The comfortable mix of mansions, fine homes, and grand cottages adds appeal to these friendly neighborhoods, which are highly sought after by home buyers.

After 1909, the year Standard Oil came to town, developers built many homes, mostly double shotguns, bungalows, and cottages, near the refinery in North Baton Rouge. Big lots, family grocery stores, neighborhood schools, and ethnic businesses made this a flourishing part of town, but as the city spread eastward in the 1970s North Baton Rouge slipped into decline. Today, urban restoration companies are busily renovating and building homes in an effort to revitalize the area.

With the 1912 arrival of Southern University north of Baton Rouge, campus neighborhoods like Zion City and Southern Heights sprang to life. Still farther north is Central, a rural area boasting large, upscale homes with an acre or more of land. Many Baton Rougeans commute from country neighborhoods near the small cities of Baker, Zachary, and, a jaunt beyond, St. Francisville.

Baton Rouge's grand homes were built in a variety of styles reflecting America's traditional architectural tastes, among others Greek Revival, Colonial, Victorian, and Queen Anne. A few Acadian-style homes and plantations were here, but for the most part, the city's early French and Spanish homes were lost to the passage of time and bombardment by Union gunboats during the Civil War.

In the 1950s, A. Hays Town, a genteel architect from Cajun country, began to design homes embodying Louisiana's French and Spanish architectural traditions. His remarkably beautiful houses, built with salvaged materials, in many ways restored Baton Rouge to its cultural roots. While turning wood craftsmanship into an art, he gave Baton Rouge a unique architectural identity that today shapes the designs of nearly every builder and developer in the city.

As a young man, Town admired the warm, open homes of the Creoles and Acadians: they were simple, practical, and yet lovely. In the hot, humid climate, Creole-Acadian cottages were raised on brick piers to protect them from floods and to allow air currents to flow underneath. Breezes flowed into the cottages through French doors and windows opening onto wide front and back galleries. Steep, overhanging roofs shaded the galleries and, when it rained, allowed people to open their doors and windows for cool, fresh air.

Fascinated by Louisiana's rustic, rural architecture, Town was the first to design homes with indigenous materials like deep-swamp cypress beams, heart-of-pine floor planks, old bricks, hand-turned columns, heavy oak mantles, carved sunburst transoms, louvered shutters, and other artifacts salvaged from old homes, warehouses, and sugar mills. His designs, gleaned from long walks along the streets of New Orleans, France, Spain, and Italy, added the Mediterranean and Caribbean architectural details that evoked the magic and mystery of early Louisiana and her roots in the Latin

Baton Rouge's grand homes were built in a variety of styles reflecting America's traditional architectural tastes, among others Greek Revival, Colonial, Victorian, and Queen Anne. *Photo by Philip Gould*

world: arched windows, ivy-bedecked French balconies, Spanish courtyard fountains, brick and flagstone floors, giant urns, sugar kettles, and, among other things, steepled brick pigeonnaires that are used here as children's playhouses or to store garden tools.

These details struck a responsive chord in Baton Rougeans. People loved the warmth, quality, and durability of the old materials as well as the simple, distinctive beauty of Louisiana's ancestral homes. Comfortable yet aesthetic, they seem to grow up out of the landscape.

Many Baton Rouge homes incorporate the area's Caribbean roots in their architecture and decoration.
Photo by Philip Gould

Not only homeowners, but also Louisiana craftsmen, builders, and developers have benefitted from the vision of this acclaimed designer. "Hays had the ability to orchestrate the craftsmen and natural materials like the words of a poem," says Kevin Harris, an architect serving on the board of the Foundation for Historical Louisiana. "The result was a magic that captured the joy of all the makers."

Millwork shops retooled their machinery to run moldings to Town's specifications. In the 1960s and '70s, architects, builders, and developers copied fragments of his style, as seen in the subdivisions most popular with newcomers: in the eastern part of the city, Sherwood Forest, Lake Sherwood, Shenandoah; and Oak Hills to the south.

The 1983 publication of "The Architectural Style of A. Hays Town" gave designers ready access to his concepts, which his protegees imitate with considerable success. Other designers express these architectural elements in an appealing, eclectic blend found nowhere else. Town is single-handedly responsible for upgrading the look of speculative homes built in Baton Rouge and for defining the aesthetic standards to which many architects still aspire.

Jefferson Place, Bocage, The Lake at White Oak, White Oak Landing, the beautiful Highland Road area, which opened to development in the mid-1980s, and scattered neighborhoods throughout the city boast spectacular homes designed by Hays Town and his talented coterie. His style, a singular form of Louisiana Colonial Revival, is now the preferred tradition in Baton Rouge.

The 1,000-acre Country Club of Louisiana, built around a Jack Nicklaus championship golf course, spurred the development of many lovely subdivisions along Highland Road. A gated community, the Country Club offers homeowners every imaginable amenity, from walking and jogging trails to tennis, swimming, and golf. It is a self-contained village with an

A. Hays Town, a genteel architect from Cajun country, came onto the Baton Rouge scene in the 1950s and is credited with restoring the city to its cultural roots through his designs that incorporate traditions of the Creoles and Acadians. *Photo by Philip Gould*

Winding along the City Park Lakes and University Lakes are magnificent, show-piece homes ranking as some of the most expensive in the city.
Photo by Philip Gould

antebellum clubhouse, twenty-five acres of common grounds and fourteen miles of roads. Homes in the Country Club are built for $300,000 to $3 million.

Colonial Revival architecture in the Country Club, as well as in the small, intimate neighborhoods on Highland Road, includes raised Creole or Acadian homes, European French country, European French chateau, and creative combinations of all three styles. The French country style features a steep, hipped slate roof, batten shutters, crank-out casement windows, and stucco made to look like stone. The chateau home is more formal, with a mansard roof, arched windows, and a large entrance.

Newer homes, regardless of location, feature large bathrooms and kitchens, breakfast areas and, thanks to Hays Town, airy 10-foot ceilings. Old materials are still being used, especially to give warmth and character to rooms, although with architectural salvage running low in Louisiana, supplies often come from other states. When they are not available, craftsmen use some of Town's clever tricks to make them look worn with age. Chains are used to dent new mantle pieces and rich stains serve to antique new woods.

Hardly anyone, however, attends to details the way Town always did, down to mixing paints to get just the right wall colors, searching antique stores for period furnishings, selecting paintings and their frames, and, on occasion, completing his living work of art with a faithful German shepherd or two.

It is interesting to note that building trends have circled back to the city's ancestral lands along Highland Road, an ancient "high land" ridge curving above the 17,000-acre Spanish Lake Basin. The French, Spanish, and Acadian architectural styles used by Town were adapted from dwelling places built by these early cultures throughout South Louisiana. It is their exquisite architecture that Town revived.

Enjoy a Sunday drive along Highland Road to admire these beautiful new homes, located in single-street and cul-de-sac neighborhoods meandering along oak-shaded Highland Road and winding down Old Perkins past Bayou Manchac into Ascension Parish.

Building trends have circled back to the city's ancestral lands along Highland Road, an ancient "high land" ridge curving above the Spanish Lake Basin.
Photo by Philip Gould

Garden district residents showcase their lovely homes with lush native plants like sweet olive, mock orange, gardenias, camellias, Louisiana iris, and Southern magnolia. *Photo by Philip Gould*

City history is quite literally built into the homes of Baton Rouge.
Photo by Philip Gould

Chapter 8

Education and Research: A2Z

Baton Rouge's blue ribbon schools produce winners, from opera singers and Olympic gold medalists to the first female aviator at West Point and the first African-American to chair the Federal Reserve Board. From people to pioneering research, contributions made by educators span the globe and make the capital city a better place to live.

Educational excellence has been a tradition here since 1868, when a priest at the present-day St. Joseph's Cathedral asked the Sisters of St. Joseph of Medaille to come up from New Orleans to care for children in the city orphanage. Once they got here, the good sisters saw the need for a school and opened St. Joseph's Academy. It is now an award-winning girls school with a college preparatory curriculum producing more than a dozen National Merit Scholars each year.

St. Joseph's Academy and the all-male Catholic High School, established in 1894 by the Brothers of the Sacred Heart, graduate students destined for career success, civic leadership and, in many cases, Ivy League colleges. These two schools, along with Episcopal and a public school, Baton Rouge Magnet High, have twice won the coveted National School of Excellence (Blue Ribbon School) Award from the U.S. Office of Education.

Baton Rouge education is making steady strides with the assistance of citizens, business, and government working in partnership. *Photo by Philip Gould*

Baton Rouge's history of private schools has given rise to more than forty of them. Seventeen Catholic schools, five Episcopal schools and non-denominational religious schools such as Christian Life Academy, The Dunham School, and Parkview Baptist strive to nurture the "whole child" through strong academics, honors, and advanced placement courses, a wide array of clubs and sports, community service programs, and attention to spiritual and moral values. These schools are open to children of any or no religious affiliation.

Episcopal schools educate two thousand students enrolled in four elementary campuses and at Episcopal, a K-12 school serving one thousand students. All of Episcopal's students are college bound, many of them to Harvard, Princeton, Yale, and Duke by virtue of accelerated academics and courses in the classics and liberal arts.

Smaller secular schools like Millerville Academy and The Runnels School offer strong basic academics, accelerated and honors courses, arts programs, and the reduced class sizes that enable teachers to spend more time with each child.

Baton Rouge offers educational opportunities for everyone, with choices ranging from traditional academic study to vocational training and hands-on learning environments. *Photo by Philip Gould*

Within the public school system, several top-notch schools produce distinguished students, dozens of National Merit Finalists and Semi-Finalists, more than $10 million in scholarships, and student ACT and SAT scores exceeding state and national averages.

Many elementary schools use interdisciplinary, collaborative instruction to excite student creativity and engender a love for learning.

Baton Rouge Magnet High School offers students the chance to run the world's only AM and FM radio stations at a high school. *Photo by Philip Gould*

Another leading high school, Scotlandville Magnet High, is a math and science magnet with a strong arts program and an engineering focus. Engineering students get an early start in science and technical fields. Seniors earn college credits in computers, drafting, electronics, and technical writing, to name a few, and enjoy visits by guest speakers, field trips to businesses, and workdays with engineers.

Public schools struggle with many of the same challenges that plague the rest of America, but here, thousands of community volunteers step in to guide students and enhance instruction in 102 public schools (three of which are excellent independent charter schools operated by entrepreneurs). Spearheading this community involvement is the non-profit Volunteers in Public Schools (VIPS).

One VIPS program, Partners in Education, co-sponsored by the school system and The Chamber of Greater Baton Rouge, has made a world of difference in public schools. Business and industry adopters provide everything from science awards and lab equipment to new and recycled computers. Their employees paint and repair school buildings, plant trees, tutor students, hook up schools to the Internet, give classroom lectures, and support educators whenever help is needed.

Another community effort, the Academic Distinction Fund (ADF), gives competitive grants for innovative classroom projects and for programs with schoolwide impact. Since 1989, the ADF has invested more than $600,000 in nearly eight hundred projects. They range from outdoor discovery stations and building a rain forest to peer tutoring and skits on conflict resolution. The non-profit Baton Rouge Area Foundation manages a $3 million endowment fund raised privately by the ADF within the community.

Progressive teachers in public schools, as in private schools, use whole language, math manipulatives, and hands-on science, along with computer instruction and arts enrichment by visiting artists. In middle schools, team teaching and advisor-advisee programs enable teachers to collaborate on interdisciplinary units and give students more individual attention. For adolescents, the mentoring and interpretive, exploratory approach to learning helps smooth the transition to high school.

Magnet programs offer advanced courses, expanded electives, and appealing programs for college-bound students. Studies spring to life in these quality schools, with programs in accelerated academics; composition/writing and communications technology; foreign language and international studies; computers, math, and science; and science and technology.

Arts education begins at the Baton Rouge Center for Visual and Performing Arts and continues at Broadmoor Middle Magnet and Baton Rouge Magnet High School. Baton Rouge Magnet High, also an academics magnet, is a model school with advanced placement courses, an orchestra and jazz band, the world's only AM and FM radio stations at a high school, a wide array of regular arts courses, and music, art, and drama classes for students designated by the state as talented.

Matching funds for ADF grants come from the Louisiana Education Quality Support Fund (LEQSF), a trust fund created with investment interest from a 1986 offshore oil settlement. LEQSF grants have averaged $28 million per year in recent years and are steadily improving Louisiana education. In East Baton Rouge Parish, the program's competitive grants enhance all subject areas, bring in artists to work with students, improve instructional techniques, send teachers to workshops for hands-on math and science, and implement model programs for at-risk students. One major block grant to the Catholic Diocese of Baton Rouge connected fifteen thousand students to the Scholastic Network, a global telecommunications program.

The close relationship between educators and the business community bodes well for public schools and undergirds the city's boom economy. According to experts, economic prosperity can only be sustained by a capable workforce that pays taxes, boosts sales revenues and raises the quality of life for everyone. It is this young, dynamic workforce that will "grow" the city by attracting new businesses.

Baton Rouge is ready for them. The Chamber of Greater Baton Rouge, in linking the school system and the business community, is at the center of several workforce development programs. One of them, the Baker High Workforce Development Academy, teaches welding, plumbing, electrical, and other technical trades. Short-term programs held in different schools give students a jump-start into automotive, banking, and finance careers, to name a few.

Baton Rouge's public and private schools produce distinguished students who are recognized for their excellence as National Merit scholars, win millions of dollars in scholarships, and whose ACT and SAT scores exceed state and national averages. *Photo by Philip Gould*

The LSU System, composed of eight institutions on ten campuses in five cities, attracts students from all fifty states and more than 120 foreign countries.
Photo by Philip Gould

After high school, young people study for vo-tech careers at the Louisiana Technical College in Baton Rouge or any of three technical colleges located in the adjacent Ascension, Iberville and West Baton Rouge parishes. LEQSF grants, as part of a program to improve secondary schools, have purchased state-of-the-art equipment for the technical colleges. The grants also fund Quickstart projects that train students for jobs specific to incoming or expanding businesses.

The Chamber, school system, and business community are also designing progressive training programs for high school dropouts, unemployed young people, and adult workers in need of retraining. Easily the most innovative is a training camp for at-risk youth located on three hundred beautiful acres in the nearby countryside of Carville. Ultimately, the campus will accommodate one thousand young people ages fourteen to twenty-four. While living there, they will undergo aptitude testing and job training, prepare for a Graduate Equivalency Diploma and connect with waiting jobs.

The new Baton Rouge Community College bridges the gap from school to work by offering vo-tech education, adult job retraining, and associate degrees in arts and science for transfer to four-year baccalaureate colleges and universities.

Back in 1869, the year after St. Joseph's Academy opened, the present-day Louisiana State University and Agricultural and Mechanical College celebrated its first commencement and received its first research grant: to do a geological survey of Louisiana.

Since then, LSU has produced, quite literally, a wealth of information for the state by surveying lands and the Gulf of Mexico, and by making strides in petroleum engineering and chemical research. This knowledge helped bring forth Louisiana's massive petrochemical industry, and with it, a city of chemists and engineers generating private research shared with LSU and with Southern University and A&M College.

LSU, a land-grant and sea-grant university, is the state's comprehensive research institute and the only Research-1 university in the mid-South. The LSU System, composed of eight institutions on ten campuses in five cities, attracts students from all fifty states and more than 120 foreign countries.

The LSU campus is picturesque, extending from the east bank of the Mississippi River over two thousand acres. The main campus, built on a 650-acre plateau, consists of red-roofed tan buildings designed in the Renaissance architectural style of northern Italy. A campanile towers over the distinctive campus and its huge old live oak trees.

More than twenty-eight thousand students attend the Baton Rouge campus, which is home to the LSU Agricultural Center, the Paul M. Hebert Law Center, an Assembly Center used for entertainment and sporting events, and a massive athletic complex. LSU's scholars and artists contribute literature, history, art, science, and technology to the community, while its art galleries, museums, and libraries preserve the state's rich cultural heritage.

Distinguished members of the research faculty attract top-quality students and more than $70 million in grants for pure and applied research. Through the years, LSU research has yielded one hundred patents. At any given time, more than fourteen hundred sponsored research projects are underway. Geology, physics, engineering, and material science are high-focus programs.

LSU researchers collaborate on projects in thirty-five institutes, centers for advanced study, specialized units, and various state and federal governmental units with offices and laboratories on campus. Two world-class research facilities, the Pennington Biomedical Research Center and the LSU-directed Center for Advanced Microstructures and Devices (CAM-D), are located in other parts of the city and draw heavily on the scientific talent bank at the university.

The largest, most diverse centers produce high-impact work that attracts multiple grants. LSU's Coastal Studies Institute, in the forefront of deep-water research, is studying oil seeps and gas hydrates on the continental slope to learn more about untapped oil and gas reservoirs. Its Earth Scan Laboratory captures environmental data from earth-viewing satellites and monitors storms for emergency preparedness centers; coastal fog for industries; and conditions in coastal and estuarine waters for fisheries management.

The Center for Coastal, Energy and Environmental Resources combines the mind-power of Coastal Studies researchers with that of six other prominent institutes, all of which are working on technologies vital to the nation's needs. One of these, the Institute for Environmental Studies, a research and academic unit, graduates students with master's degrees in divisions including toxicology and environmental planning and management.

These LSU graduates, employed by industrial plants and private consulting firms across the globe, help clean up the environment here by enacting controls that assist industries in meeting federal standards. Institute researchers development environmental solutions. One scientist was among the world's first to design microbes for environmental waste remediation and holds several patents on "designer bugs." Other researchers have developed a portable field monitor to detect toxic pollutants in land, sea, and air.

LSU scientists are involved in virtually every field of cutting edge research, from genetic immunization of animal tissue in the LSU School of Veterinary Medicine to embryo transfer and embryo splitting in the College of Agriculture. While civil engineers devise new ways to take utilities underground and electrical engineers work with CAM-D on new physics for high-speed electronic components, studies by the Washington D.C.-based LSU National Ports and Waterways Institute benefit Louisiana and the world.

LSU economic development programs directly fuel the city's growth. Through the Community University Partnership, faculty members guide neighborhoods in architectural restoration, job service programs, and technical assistance to low-income businesses. The Louisiana Business & Technology Center, originally a joint venture with the Chamber of Commerce and now part of LSU's E.J. Ourso College of Business Administration, is a business incubator, assists entrepreneurs in business start-up, and operates the Louisiana Technology Transfer Office at NASA's John C. Stennis Space Center to procure business opportunities for Louisiana companies.

LSU scientists are involved in virtually every field of cutting edge research, from genetic immunization of animal tissue in the LSU School of Veterinary Medicine to embryo transfer and embryo splitting in the College of Agriculture. Pictured below, veterinary students prepare a racehorse for X-ray.

Photo by Philip Gould

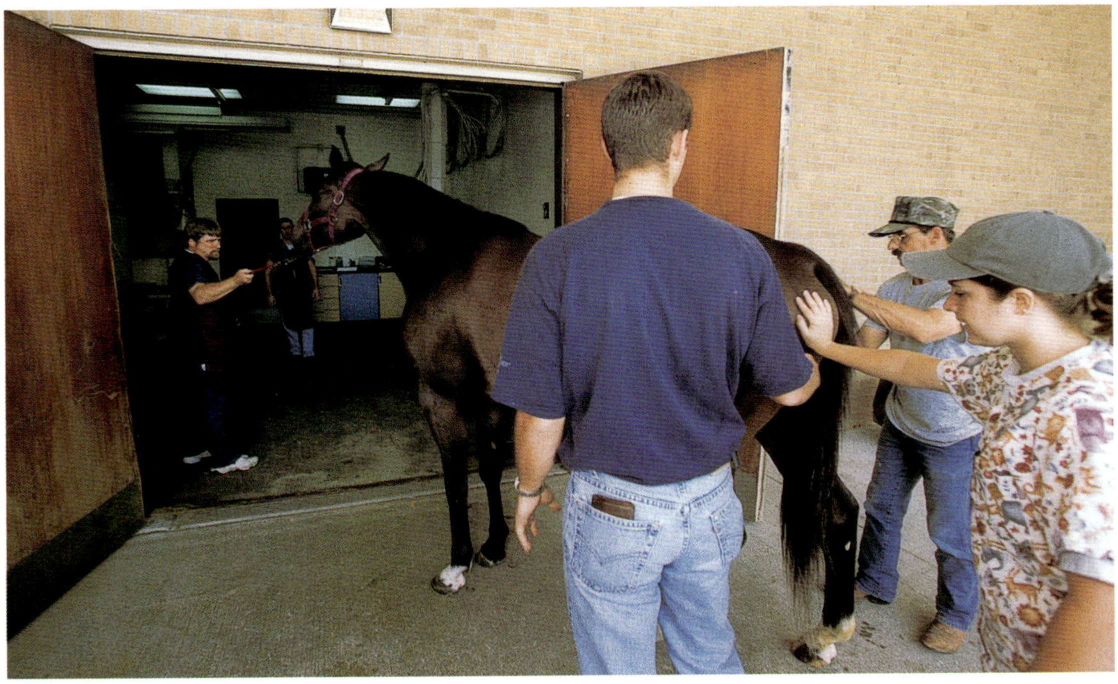

Southern University claims a unique identity as the largest African-American university in the United States, and the only black education system.
Photo by Philip Gould

Several leading research centers relate to the humanities. The T. Harry Williams Center for Oral History, named after an LSU political science professor who wrote "Huey Long," a Pulitzer-Prize winning book based on oral histories, reaches into the city and state to learn about the past. Unlike other such centers, this one also trains high school students as future oral historians.

The U.S. Civil War Center, the only comprehensive Civil War center in America, combines scholarly research with the creation of a database networking information from American universities and institutions. The center was founded by LSU English professor David Madden, author or editor of nearly fifty books and a Civil War novel, *Sharpshooter*, which was recently nominated for a Pulitzer Prize.

Some research projects at Southern University and A&M College link to LSU research projects, but most arise out of Southern's unique identity as the largest African-American university in the U.S. and the only black education system.

Chartered in 1880, Southern was recognized as a land-grant college in 1891 and, in 1912, moved here from New Orleans. The university's lovely campus, located on Scott's Bluff overlooking the Mississippi River, may occupy the original site of the red stick, dripping with bloody fish heads, which gave Baton Rouge its name in 1699. A riverfront sculpture by the late Frank Hayden, a Southern University professor, was placed on the bluff in 1976, when a city bicentennial commission held commemorative ceremonies there.

The main campus, extending over 512 acres, is situated on the largest bend in the Mississippi River. A crevasse in the bend flows into a deep ravine which rambles through the campus and feeds the scenic Lake Kernan. Two buildings on the lake, the Smith-Brown Student Union and J.B. Cade Library, reflect the light modern to contemporary architecture of the campus.

A few miles away are an additional 370 acres used for agricultural research.

Some 55 percent of all graduates pursue careers in nursing, business, English, education, and social science, attracted to SU by its strong outreach programs and research centers invested in the fields of health, sickle cell disease, African-American studies, business, and economic development.

National and international students are drawn to Southern's School of Public Policy and several undergraduate programs recognized as national models. One example is the School of Nursing, which operates a health van, the Jag Mobile, in service to citizens of the inner city and outlying areas. SU was the nation's first university to offer an undergraduate degree in urban forestry and a dam safety program in engineering. Its law center is the most diverse in America, with 60 percent black and 40 percent white enrollees.

Like LSU, Southern educates young minds in cutting edge technology and strengthens economic growth locally and globally. The Center for Small Farm Research assists low-income farmers in Louisiana, while other centers foster small business start-up in depressed areas of the city, in rural parishes and along the Delta. One research center works with USAID on international development projects and outreach in Zaire, democratization in Zambia, and education in Jamaica and South Africa. The Center for Energy and Environmental Studies networks a multidisciplinary team working on local environmental challenges.

Southern's physics department includes a world authority on superconductors and the nationally recognized Timbuktu Academy, which sends math and science scholars from area middle and high schools to do summer internships with scientists at MIT and other universities. The Timbuktu Academy, named after a famed African city of scientists, won the nation's first Presidential Award for Excellence in Science, Mathematics, and Engineering Mentoring.

Just as LSU's geo-surveys and petroleum research paved the way for the city's petrochemical economy back in the 1800s, so does pure and applied research in math, science, and engineering today generate the critical mass of brainpower needed to attract clean, high-tech industries to Baton Rouge.

Southern University's School of Nursing operates a health van, dubbed the "Jag Mobile", in service to citizens of the inner city and outlying areas, giving nursing students valuable hands-on experience. *Photo by Philip Gould*

The LEQSF or, in higher education, Board of Regents Support Fund, pours upwards of $28 million per year into several far-reaching programs designed to improve education and stimulate competitive research. Board of Regents grants fund an endowed chairs and professorships programs; recruit the state's most promising scholars, researchers, and graduate students; and fund competitive grants through a research and development program that stimulates economic growth. BoR grants serve as seed money for matching private and federal grants that are opening windows of opportunity for Baton Rouge.

One $800,000 Board of Regents grant has stimulated a total $2.4-million grant matched

Not all learning takes place in a classroom. Baton Rouge youngsters enjoy hands-on learning experiences with field trips to such places as the Rural Life Museum (above), where D.J. Alleman, Jr., demonstrates the art of pirogue construction; and the USS Kidd (right), a restored and preserved battleship moored on the Mississippi Riverbank.
Photos by Philip Gould

by the Department of Energy, private industry, and nine Louisiana universities. Working in clusters, the universities focus on several different research areas. One project uses lasers to fabricate new semiconductor materials for use in computer chips. Another employs high-tech equipment to design and study new rust-resistant metal coatings. Both are applicable to the local economy.

LEQSF investment interest funds, which increase each year until offshore revenues reach $2 billion, are helping to guide the city and state into its economic future.

One major field of research, astrophysics, is a focus of the Louisiana Board of Regents and is receiving attention and funding from NASA. Faculty members at LSU and Southern co-direct a Louisiana Space Consortium (LaSpace) consisting of seventeen colleges and universities, business and industry partners, and non-profit organizations working together to boost Louisiana's involvement in aerospace R&D, education, and economic development.

NASA and the Board of Regents are also funding astrophysics research cluster projects involving LSU, Southern, and other universities. Scientists are constructing an experiment for a high altitude research balloon to be launched in New Mexico; it will measure the highest energy cosmic rays from supernova remnants. Aerospace propulsion experiments involve computer simulation modeling and a combustion chamber used for fuel efficiency experiments. Southern and LSU are also working together on balloon observations of the university through x-rays and gamma rays.

In separate research, LSU scientists are devising flight experiments for the International Space Station in the year 2005. At Southern University, an undergraduate aerospace degree will, no doubt, draw its math and science scholars from the Timbuktu Academy. They will be ably trained by aerospace researchers at Southern and LSU and by global scientists attracted to the metro area by a $105 million Laser Interferometer Gravitational-Wave Observatory (LIGO) in nearby Livingston Parish.

Funded by the National Science Foundation, LIGO facilities being built in the metro area and in Hanford, Washington, connect scientists at LSU, the California Institute of Technology, and MIT in a search for answers about the origins of the universe.

Vibrant and exciting, Baton Rouge research works hand-in-hand with education to stimulate

the entire city. The new Highland Road Park Observatory keeps young eyes on the heavens with telescope stargazing, campfire lectures, workshops, and computerized remote controls used to record nighttime images and transport them to classrooms at Southern, LSU and, eventually, public schools across the parish.

With its profusion of technical minds and humanitarian hearts, Baton Rouge is rich in education. Many attractions are educational by nature, from swamp tours to the Rural Life Museum, from LASC's space flight simulator to its one-of-a-kind planetarium and space theater.

People hungry for knowledge enjoy free literature classes at the city's main library or math tutoring at one of twelve library branches. College credits in every discipline, including programs originated here for the people of Louisiana, are available year-round on WLPB-TV, the statewide public broadcasting station.

While not perfect, Baton Rouge education is making steady strides with the assistance of citizens, business, and government working in partnership. Their keen minds and caring, creative solutions will ably prepare Baton Rougeans for success in the new millennium. ⚜

Chapter 9

Visions of the Future

Someone once said that the best way to build a good life, or by extension, a successful city, is to envision the construction of a house. Devise a plan, work on it day by day, and include only the attributes, or building materials, that will ensure quality in the structure.

That's how Baton Rougeans are building their city. Working together, citizens are drawing blueprints, hammering, nailing, sheetrocking, painting, roofing, and landscaping everything from the arts to urban restoration. As a result, Baton Rouge will weather time and change with strength and grace.

Back in the 1980s, during the years of the oil bust, many disheartened people left Baton Rouge for what seemed to be more successful cities. Many of those families returned, partly because they missed the good people back home, and partly because, no matter how green the grass on the other side, these are remarkably fertile fields with plenty of room to set down roots, build, and claim a stake in the future.

As serendipity would have it, just when Baton Rougeans most needed to participate, a new mayor, Tom Ed McHugh, opened the doors of city government to shared leadership. It was a revolutionary move and, as McHugh realized, the only way to effectively, and quickly, resolve urban challenges—that is, with the cooperative involvement of the entire community.

Since its earliest days, Baton Rougeans have faced the future with courage and strength, forging a city of rich cultural diversity and opportunity for all.
Photo by Philip Gould

In 1989, a group of nine "civic warriors"—attorneys, realtors, industry workers, civil rights activists, ministers, environmentalists, and others -- came together as the Baton Rouge Town Meeting Committee and blossomed into a model program with city-wide participation. The notion of shared leadership gained momentum as crowds of people turned up at town meetings to discuss their most urgent concerns: air pollution, children's needs, workforce development, crime, racism, public education, and citizenship.

New leaders emerged at each meeting, along with active, hard-working committees. Change came quickly.

The first town meeting, "Smog Talk," brought together industrial leaders and environmentalists. Their plan became an EPA national model. The alliance formed a group called Baton Rouge Earth Day, which created the largest Earth Day celebration in the South and the second largest in the nation. Since 1990, there has also been a significant improvement in air quality.

Baton Rouge combines all that is best about its past with a vision for all it could be in the future to devise a blueprint for future growth.
Photo by Philip Gould

Today, groups like Baton Rouge Green, Friends of Environmental Education, the Louisiana Environmental Action Network,

Baton Rouge is fast emerging as a city leader with its heart in children. Innovative programs that have captured national attention include the President's Summit for America's Future (now America's Promise), Children's Coalition, and Community Action for Children.
Photos by Philip Gould

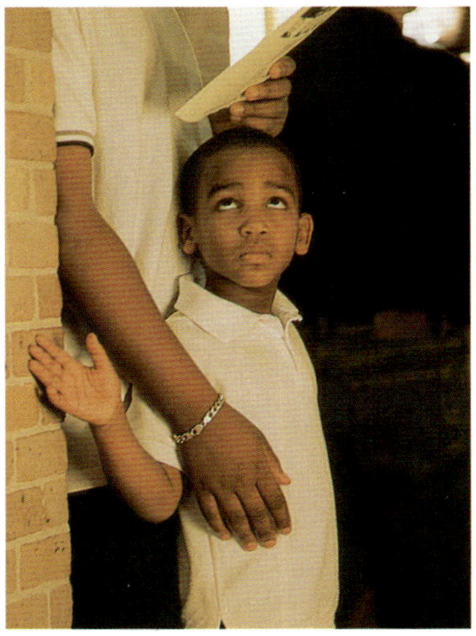

Louisiana Nature Conservancy, Bluff Swamp Wildlife Refuge, and many others are working to protect, preserve, restore, and beautify Baton Rouge and the state. Much remains to be done and will be.

The next town meeting gave rise to a Children's Coalition that worked to unite eighty youth-serving agencies, recruit and educate an excellent school board, and lay the groundwork for an uptake group, Community Action for Children (CAC). CAC consolidated the plans and resources of city-parish government, the school system, a Children's Coalition, United Way, School-Based Health Clinics, and the Academic Distinction Fund to ensure caring, safety, health services, a good education, and service opportunities to the children of the metro area. In late 1997, more than 350 community leaders attended the unveiling of CAC's blueprint for the future of Baton Rouge's young people.

Another landmark town meeting, "Where Is The 'U' in Public Education?", led to school town meetings held at all 102 public schools in the parish. School Improvement Teams include parents, school staff, students, and business and community members. While SITs define and activate plans to upgrade education on individual campuses, the Louisiana Department of Education is mobilizing an ambitious accountability initiative to bring all public schools to or beyond the highest national standards.

Baton Rouge's team efforts led the Ohio-based Kettering Foundation to declare it a model research city of effective democratic politics. In 1996, because of its history of public dialogue and participation, Baton Rouge was selected as one of 140 cities invited to attend the President's Summit for America's

Future, now America's Promise, led by retired U.S. General Colin Powell to draw attention to the needs of children.

Baton Rouge is fast emerging as a city leader with its heart in children. The city's plan for America's Promise is now the model for the state. And in a televised C-SPAN special on nationwide efforts for children, the local CAC plan was highlighted and Baton Rouge was named one of four model cities in the United States.

Town meetings, though they may sound tame, are courageous efforts to effect change. Their essence is "people-power," says Jan Bernard, who guided the process as assistant chief administrative officer to Mayor-President McHugh.

"In town meetings," she explains, "people discover each other and unite to build a better community. Personal passion brings them to the table. Sometimes that's anger, sometimes that's love for a child. Regardless, it's a desire to act together."

An active program of Town Meetings addresses varied concerns of Baton Rouge citizens and encourages individual involvement. Topics have included "Where is the 'U' in Public Education?", "What Color is Community?", and "Crime: Have You Had Enough?"
Photo by Philip Gould

Groups such as Baton Rouge Earth Day, Baton Rouge Green, Friends of Environmental Education, the Louisiana Environmental Action Network, Louisiana Nature Conservancy, Bluff Swamp Wildlife Refuge, and many others are working to protect, preserve, restore, and beautify Baton Rouge and the state.
Photo by Philip Gould

One town meeting, "What Color is Community?" successfully tackled the difficult subject of race relations. A series of active committees sprang out of a follow-up conference, "The Second Mile," which continues to bring people together to find ways to remedy racial injustice.

The Young Women's Christian Association, pioneers since the late 1960s in eliminating racism, the Federation of Churches and Synagogues, the Catholic Diocese of Baton Rouge, and many other groups are deeply involved in community efforts to build bridges between races and religions. Interracial efforts by churches, the Baton Rouge Council on Human Relations, Project Harmony, 100 Black Men, 100 Black Women, and many other leading coalitions actively work to forge mutual understanding, acceptance, and respect.

"Crime: Have You Had Enough?" was another tough issue for Baton Rougeans. This town meeting prompted some five hundred neighborhood and regional community meetings, crime-fighting initiatives, and the demolition of more than one thousand deteriorated, drug-riddled city properties. Results include a dramatic decrease in crime and random violence, the establishment of a drug court, and ten community-based organizations that continue to address drug problems and crime.

Baton Rouge government has a progressive new way of doing business. In 1991, the city-parish implemented the Total Quality Movement (TQM), creating an internal Quality and Employee Development Office and introducing an independent program of awards given annually to highly productive TQM businesses in the nine-parish economic region. City-parish offices have won several of these awards. All in all, the Quality program has taught local government to plan better, improve its internal processes, and hold community meetings on city development.

Baton Rouge is fast emerging as a city leader. While Quality principles and the results of town meetings ripple out to effect growth and change, civic leaders are busily building the city with assistance from the next generation.

Today, the Baton Rouge Town Meeting Committee, expanded to a 24-member steering committee, is training three hundred volunteers a year to foster public dialogue. The trainees will create new initiatives and sharpen

blueprints by the original Town Meeting Committee, such as Create Baton Rouge, an arts and cultural planning initiative. The Baton Rouge Center for World Affairs, a spinoff of the International Relations Commission and parent to the International Heritage Festival, welcomes foreign consuls and visiting business people and shows them all that Baton Rouge celebrates.

Baton Rouge celebrates its diversity most of all and the willing volunteers who so readily step up to the plate. Literally thousands of adults and teenagers have signed on with Volunteer Baton Rouge to mobilize city resources and actively build community partnerships. And each year, a Chamber of Commerce program, Leadership Baton Rouge, trains thirty new city leaders. Leadership's 400-member alumni group is working on an in-depth assessment of city progress in all of its endeavors. The Baton Rouge Area Foundation, catalyst to arts, education, Plan Baton Rouge and many other master plans, also seeded Forum 35, a group of successful young business people devoted to nurturing city growth.

All of these efforts are in harmony with the old French custom of the charrette, in which an architect works on-site with a land owner to design and landscape just the right home.

Baton Rougeans are indeed building good, quality lives for themselves and the world. In these years of the city's tricentennial, one can only marvel at their eager willingness to design their futures and at the rapidity with which lasting progress, through partnership, can and is being made. ⚜

Baton Rouge is fast emerging as a leading city. Civic leaders are busily building the city with assistance from the community, and from the next generation.
Photo by Philip Gould

Part 2

Industry, Manufacturing, and Distribution

Uniroyal Chemical Company, Inc.

The next time you find yourself looking back at a high performance car or trying to catch a second glimpse of a lush and beautiful flower garden, you might also want to take another look at Uniroyal Chemical Company, Inc.

As a subsidiary of Crompton & Knowles Corporation, a worldwide specialty chemicals and equipment manufacturer, Uniroyal Chemical is a major supplier of rubber and specialty chemicals to both the domestic and international marketplace. The company has 21 manufacturing sites (including joint ventures) around the world with one of its largest facilities located just south of Baton Rouge in Geismar, Louisiana.

In fact, some of the very chemicals and additives which go into helping cars run better or flowers grow more beautifully, as well as hundreds of other items we see of use in our lives daily, actually got their start at the Uniroyal Chemical facility in Louisiana.

The plant first began operations in 1962 and has been expanded over 30 times. The site now covers a total of 430 acres including a river frontage of 1,800 feet.

The Geismar site was originally selected because of the area's abundant supply of natural gas, which is used as both a raw material and as fuel to operate the facility. Currently, there are 11 operating units at Uniroyal Chemical. These operating units work under three of Uniroyal Chemical's business divisions: Crop Protection; Chemicals and Polymers; and Specialty Chemicals.

What exactly are the products that Uniroyal Chemical makes? Not surprisingly, many people still associate Uniroyal Chemical with its former parent, Uniroyal, Inc., the company that made and sold tires. However, even though the two companies share a name, Uniroyal Chemical is very different.

Uniroyal Chemical doesn't make tires, but they do make many of the products that go into tires, such as *Flexzone*, a rubber chemical used to protect tires and other rubber products from deterioration.

Royalene EPDM is also used in the automotive industry. Produced at Uniroyal Chemical's Geismar manufacturing plant, it is a high-performance specialty synthetic rubber that has excellent chemical resistance, resilience, and heat aging. Those qualities make it ideal for a wide range of automotive applications including the production of hoses, belts, and weather seals.

Farmers and gardening enthusiasts also depend on various crop protection chemicals produced at Uniroyal Chemical's Geismar facility. One chemical, which is later formulated into a product called Royal MH-30 and Royal Slo-Gro, helps prevent the growth of suckers on tobacco plants and helps prevent sprouting in potatoes and onions.

Another product produced at the Louisiana site is B-Nine. When potted ornamental flowers are treated with B-Nine, their petals are compact, dense, and uniform, producing a bounteous and envious bed of healthy, long-lasting blooms.

Interestingly, many of the products manufactured at Uniroyal Chemical's Geismar facility leave the plant in a form not typically associated with chemicals. One of the plant's biggest products, synthetic rubber, is shipped out of the site in the form of dry white bales. The bales are then processed into many useful rubber products.

Improving the quality of these products and others manufactured at Uniroyal Chemical is a

never-ending process, and one that the company managers and employees take very seriously. The Geismar facility has various quality assurance programs and procedures established in every area of the plant. The company's goal is to improve product quality by the reduction of variability.

One key element of reaching this goal is called Statistical Process Control (SPC). This effort involves identifying key in-process parameters that relate to the quality and performance of the plant's products. The variability of these parameters is then closely monitored to ensure that continuous improvements in all areas are being met. Employees from all sections of the plant have been trained in SPC techniques.

Uniroyal Chemical takes seriously protecting the environment. Crompton & Knowles is

a signatory to Responsible Care, a program launched by Chemical Manufacturers Association to respond to public concerns about the manufacture and safe use of chemicals. As a participant in the program, the company is committed to the support of continuing effort to improve the industry's responsible management of chemicals and protection of the environment.

These continuing efforts include promoting emergency response planning and encouraging dialogue with local communities, protecting people and the environment by promoting the reduction and safe management of waste, and repackaging of chemicals.

But Uniroyal Chemical is not just talking about these efforts. Indeed, the Geismar facility has a long record of superior environmental performance. The company has an excellent compliance record. Recent Region VI multimedia inspections by both the Louisiana Department of Environmental Quality (LaDEQ) and the U.S. Environmental Protection Agency (EPA) were successfully met without any problems.

The company was awarded a National Performance Review Certificate from Vice President Al Gore for outstanding achievements in the U.S. EPA's 33/50 program.

In addition, the facility was honored by the state's top ranking official. Uniroyal Chemical has received the 1996, 1997, and 1998 Louisiana Governor's Award for outstanding achievements in pollution prevention. In 1997, the plant was recognized as a "Facility of the Year" by the *Environmental Protection Magazine.*

The company lists many other accomplishments. In fact, these achievements total more than 500; that's the number of salaried and contract employees working at the facility. Uniroyal Chemical is proud of its employees and supports and encourages their training, dedication, and involvement both on and off the job. The company strongly believes that its employees are the key to meeting the challenges of tomorrow.

What are those challenges? At the Geismar plant, they are continuously improving the quality of its products and services, as well as providing a safe and healthy working environment.

How do the employees help accomplish these goals? One way is by a team-based approach. In fact, the company has found that when employees come together as teams, solve real job problems, identify opportunities for improvement, and then make them happen, extraordinary things result.

Teams from the Louisiana plant have won numerous national awards, including positions among the top 18 high performing teams in the Association for Quality and Participation's National Team Excellence competition. In 1996, a team won the coveted gold medal in that event.

In addition, teams from the Geismar facility have been showcased in many national and international publications, and many companies (customers and non-customers) have even visited the plant to use this program as a benchmark for their own employee involvement.

But Uniroyal Chemical employees are not just using teams to win national competitions. They are also transferring their skills into the community.

One activity the company and its employees and contractors find most rewarding is the Adopt-A-School program. Uniroyal Chemical employees work with students and teachers at Dutchtown Primary and Middle Schools on numerous projects. From judging school science fairs and other related contests to providing reading and tutoring programs, Uniroyal Chemical places a high value on education and the kind of community our children will one day inherit.

Other voluntary employee efforts support the United Way, Cooperative Office of Education (COE), Junior Achievement, and Dreams Come True. Employees volunteer their time away from work as coaches, school volunteers, Scoutmasters, deputy sheriffs, volunteer firemen, school board committee members, emergency responders, and 4-H Club advisors.

At Uniroyal Chemical's Geismar plant, employee involvement works because of the commitment and dedication of its employees. After all, it is their involvement in continuously seeking the best that allows Uniroyal Chemical to better serve its community and its customers and to ultimately maintain its competitive position in the global marketplace. ✤

The Dow Chemical Company Louisiana Operations

Over 4,000 visitors tour Dow's Plaquemine facility annually, including students and teachers who job shadow as part of the company's educational outreach program.

Proud to be a part of the Greater Baton Rouge Metropolitan Area, The Dow Chemical Company's Louisiana Operations is an active participant in the local community, providing jobs, economic stability, and a strong commitment to maintain and enhance the quality of life for every resident.

Established in 1956, Dow's Louisiana Operations is one of the largest petrochemical facilities in Louisiana. The 1,500 acre facility produces more than 50 different products which are shipped all over the world and serve as the "building blocks" for hundreds of items used everyday. Some of the consumer products made with chemicals produced at the Louisiana site include soaps and detergents, food additives, cosmetics and shampoos, diaper liners, non-oil base paints, pharmaceuticals, and herbicides.

Dow's Louisiana Operations is located on Louisiana Highway 1 in Plaquemine, in both Iberville and West Baton Rouge Parishes. Nearby, in Assumption Parish, Dow is part owner of a fractionation plant with Koch Hydrocarbon and the company also operates a brine production facility where a saturated brine solution is mined from the Napoleonville salt dome located 1,000 feet below the surface.

Providing employment for more than 3,000 employees and contract workers, Dow is the largest employer in Iberville and West Baton Rouge Parishes. The company is also one of the largest taxpayers in Assumption, Iberville, and West Baton Rouge Parishes, and supports other local and state companies by purchasing more than $209.5 million in equipment and supplies from Louisiana businesses.

But by far, one of Dow's most impressive contributions to the state and local area is the company's extensive community involvement. Louisiana Operations employees have a long history of helping the community through volunteerism, and the company encourages, supports, and recognizes employees who volunteer their time, skills, and talents to solve problems, assist others, and make the community a better place to live.

In 1998 alone, over 20,000 hours were volunteered by employees to support Dow's community outreach programs. What did these employees do? They gave their time to benefit 40 different activities in the community. These activities included: assisting 600 needy children in Iberville and West Baton Rouge Parishes through an annual toy drive; collecting 7,000 pounds of food for area food banks; participating in the March of Dimes Walk America and the American Cancer Society Relay for Life; and giving over $580,000 to the Capital Area United Way.

Dow's efforts to enhance the local community reach many civic and charitable causes by providing $1 million in community contributions in the greater Baton Rouge area. Annual donations of more than $50,000 to nonprofit agencies in Assumption, Iberville, and West Baton Rouge Parishes are part of the Company's Community Grant Program. The company routinely donates its surplus equipment and supplies to non-profit organizations and schools, and also contributed $20,000 to the Restoration of Old City Hall in Plaquemine.

Dedicated to preserving the heritage and culture of the area, Dow has restored the 1910 Union Plantation House for company meetings and events.

Conservation and preservation projects, such as Mandalay National Wildlife Refuge, are examples of Dow's commitment to a sustainable future.

A long-time supporter of education, Dow Chemical's Louisiana Operations has been instrumental in strengthening educational opportunities for students and teachers in local schools. Annually, the company provides $24,000 in educational enhancement grants to local teachers and $28,000 in college scholarships, including two scholarships in process control technology at the Baton Rouge Community College. Dow employees regularly serve as science fair judges, guest lecturers, and career day speakers. They also serve as demonstrators for the company's Science is Phun program which provides hands-on demonstrations for 1,150 elementary school students to increase their awareness of chemistry's role in our everyday life.

Perhaps the greatest jewel of Dow's community outreach in education is the company's "Hands-On Science Program." The company has invested $440,000 for training and support of this innovative learning program in Iberville, West Baton Rouge, and East Baton Rouge schools. Designed for children in kindergarten through sixth grade, Dow's "Hands-On Science" program helps increase a student's interest in science by encouraging children to conduct experiments, make observations, and answer their own questions through experiences, not memorization.

Dow's Louisiana Operations is also very active in Junior Achievement, contributing over $7500 and eight employees to teach "Project Business" classes at local schools. The company also provides "job shadowing" opportunities for teachers. Through this "School to Work" program, teachers come to the plant and shadow Dow employees to learn which courses and skills students will need to acquire to work in the industry.

The company's High School Hazardous Material Collection Program combines Dow's support of local schools and its commitment to the environment by helping school teachers and administrators dispose of hazardous chemicals. In 1998, Dow's Louisiana Operations incinerated more than 46,000 pounds, or 23 tons, of hazardous chemicals collected from more than 400 high school and middle school chemistry laboratories in Louisiana. Dow partners with the Louisiana Chemical Association, the Louisiana Department of Environmental Quality, and Chemical Waste Management in coordinating this project, which is the only free program of its kind in the country.

Another free environmental program Dow sponsors assists residents in disposing of regular household hazardous wastes such as unused fertilizers, pesticides, pool chemicals, and household cleaners. A hundred Dow employees volunteer to collect and dispose of over 150,000 pounds of household hazardous materials from the Plaquemine and greater Baton Rouge communities during the company's annual Household Hazardous Materials Day.

Dow makes materials that go into products that make life easier.

The company's commitment to the environment is also shown in other ways not so easily measured. Like how the preservation efforts of Louisiana's coastal wetlands will be helped thanks to a $300,000 Dow grant. The gift, which also included a matching grant from the National Fish and Wildlife Federation, was given to The Nature Conservancy of Louisiana in 1992 as part of Dow's $3 million wetlands initiative called Conservation 2000. The Nature Conservancy used the donations to preserve more than 4,000 acres of Louisiana coastal wetlands. Today, the site is known as the Mandalay National Wildlife Refuge, and it provides a critical habitat for many species such as the Bald Eagle, the Peregrine Falcon, and the Alligator Snapping Turtle. Over 1 million bass and catfish fingerlings were raised in a Dow pond to replenish the Atchafalaya Basin devastated by Hurricane Andrew in cooperation with the State Department of Wildlife and Fisheries.

As a Michigan-based company, The Dow Chemical Company celebrates more than 100 years in business; the company can look back with great pride on its continuing commitment to the environment. Long recognizing that its employees and their families live in the same community where it operates, Dow, a Fortune 500 Company, has annual sales of more than $18 billion. Employees continuously work toward achieving a company goal of reducing waste and operating safely in a way that protects the environment. Here in Louisiana, Dow has achieved that goal many times over. Since 1988, the company has reduced emissions by 66 percent, and has been recognized as an OSHA Star site, one of the highest industry awards for safety, for eight consecutive years. ✤

Exxon

Of all the industries that have come to call Baton Rouge home, one in particular can be historically credited with helping to turn this sleepy southern river town into a flourishing vibrant city.

For nearly a century, Exxon and Baton Rouge have been growing and working together, both sharing a common vision of tradition and excellence. Indeed, the two have experienced many changes since Exxon's Baton Rouge Refinery first began operations as part of Standard Oil in 1909.

Back then, the city had no "skyline," horse-drawn buggies struggled through muddy streets downtown, and agriculture was the main order of business in Baton Rouge. In fact, the refinery was built on 225 acres of former cotton fields in North Baton Rouge. Even the local press marveled at the amount of money the new refinery would pump into the local economy. An editor for the *State-Times* determined the total of construction wages alone to be a sum "equivalent to at least two-thirds of the total money value of the entire cotton crop of East Baton Rouge for the year 1909."

Today, Exxon continues to reach new milestones in Baton Rouge. Over the years, the company has grown with the Capitol City, expanding to more than 3,000 acres. Exxon Company, U.S.A.; Exxon Chemical Company; and Exxon Research and Development Laboratories operate a total of nine subsidiaries in the Baton Rouge area.

At each facility, products, or the materials that go into the products we use every day, are made. The two largest facilities are the Baton Rouge Refinery and Chemical Plant; both are located on Scenic Highway by the Mississippi River. The Baton Rouge Refinery is the largest refinery in the United States, processing 473,000 barrels of crude oil per day. Interestingly, when the refinery first began operations more than 90 years ago, it could only process 1,800 barrels of crude oil per day, and could manufacture only gasoline, kerosene, and heavy fuel oil. Today, the refinery manufactures about 300 petroleum products and grades of products, including motor gasoline, diesel, jet fuel, and lubricating oils.

Exxon Community Involvement Through Employees, ExC!TE, builds houses with Habitat for Humanity.

Founded in 1940, Exxon's Chemical Plant produces products used in households and businesses, such as tape, disposable diapers, golf balls, crayons, cassette tapes, adhesive bandages, surgical gloves, and paints. As of year-end 1998, this modern petrochemical processing and manufacturing facility produced 9.7 billion pounds of petrochemical products.

Other Exxon facilities in the Baton Rouge area include the Baton Rouge Polyolefins Plant, one of the first plants in the industry to adopt Total Quality Management and achieve ISO 9000, and Exxon Research and Development Laboratories. The Baton Rouge Resin Finishing Plant, the Baton Rouge Plastics Plant, the Port Allen Lubricants Plant, the Intermediates Technology Center, and Anchorage Chemical Terminal conclude the list.

Exxon is one of the area's largest employers, providing jobs for more than 5,400 employees, including contractors. The company's annual payroll is more than $295 million. For every job Exxon creates, the company also supports six additional jobs in the community through the purchase of various goods and services from other businesses. Each year, Exxon spends almost $900 million to operate its Baton Rouge facilities. The company also provides 10 percent of the parish's tax revenue.

At Exxon, safety is a top priority. In addition to maintaining a fully trained, highly qualified emergency team 24 hours a day, seven days a week, Exxon also imposes rigorous engineering standards and operating practices at each facility. Over the years, Exxon has received numerous safety awards. Most recently, the U.S. Department of Labor's Occupational Safety and Health Administration (OSHA) recognized the Baton Rouge Plastics Plant as a Safety Through Accountability and Recognition (STAR) facility. This is the highest recognition given to an industry participant in OSHA's Voluntary Protection Program.

Every day, about 10 barges and one ocean-going tanker slide up to the Exxon dock in Baton Rouge to deliver crude oil and carry away petroleum and chemical products to all corners of the globe. One environmental improvement is the Marine Vapor Recovery system, a $15.6-million-dollar project installed at the dock to collect and destroy vapors generated during the loading of 'light" products such as gasoline and aviation fuel.

The red shirts of the Exxon Ambassadors are common sights at 10 North Baton Rouge schools where they volunteer to assist with math and science activities and at community events such as Earth Day where they perform educational demonstrations.

In addition to safety, Exxon cares about the environment. The company has long been a champion of environmentally sound processing and manufacturing techniques. Exxon was one of the first companies to implement various controls to protect Baton Rouge's natural resources. Most recently, Exxon installed the Marine Vapor Recovery system, which has decreased emissions from marine loading by 95 percent. By working with the Department of Environmental Quality and other companies, Exxon has helped develop a voluntary strategy to help preserve, protect, and restore our community's environment.

Exxon also strives to be a good corporate citizen and is working to better Baton Rouge through a partnership with education. Exxon firmly believes that the industry's competitiveness, both in the U.S. and internationally, will one day depend on today's students. That's why the company proudly supports several extensive efforts in Baton Rouge's schools designed to promote science and math education, the essential building blocks needed for careers in the petrochemical field.

Through such programs as Exxon Ambassadors, Adopt-a-School, Volunteers in Public Schools, Speakers Bureau, and Junior Achievement, Exxon employees play a big part in enhancing education in the community. By giving their time and expertise, employee volunteers benefit students through tutoring, mentoring, giving presentations, and judging science fairs.

Exxon also provides tools that help the teachers teach. The company regularly sponsors training programs for teachers on science and math subjects, and Exxon's sponsorship of WBRZ-TV's WeatherNet 2 brought fully automated weather stations, complete with computer software and lesson plans, to many area schools and the Louisiana Arts and Science Center.

The Exxon Education Foundation has also contributed more than $700,000 to the East Baton Rouge Parish school system to fund a kindergarten-through-third-grade math program that allows teachers and students to learn from hands-on computer experiences.

In addition, local community and volunteer organizations also benefit from Exxon. For years now, the company and its employees have given more than $1 million annually to the Capitol Area United Way, helping to make Exxon the agency's largest corporate contributor.

Another corporate donation of $250,000 from Exxon also helped turn a desolate, swampy area off Bluebonnet Road into a 101-acre nature refuge. Dedicated to conservation, science education, recreation, and ecotourism, the Bluebonnet Swamp has quickly become one of the area's premier attractions.

Of course, giving comes in all forms and that is something Exxon employees demonstrate almost every day. Since 1991, company employees have come together to help various groups through an organization known as ExC!TE, Exxon Community Involvement Through Employees. Whether it's picking up a hammer for Habitat for Humanity, collecting food for the Baton Rouge Food Bank, or helping citizens recycle items during the group's Monthly Recycling Day, ExC!TE is just one way employees pool their efforts to benefit the community and the environment.

As a result of these individual and corporate efforts, Exxon is today respected not only by Baton Rouge's financial community, but also by local community activists. Of course, much has changed since that simple cotton field was transformed into a prosperous industrial complex many years ago, but Exxon has remained committed to being a good corporate neighbor, proving that, by working together and growing together, great things are in store for Baton Rouge in the new century. ⚜

Exxon's Refinery and Chemical Plant in Baton Rouge, located on the Mississippi River, comprise one of the largest and most versatile petrochemical complexes in the world. From it come the petroleum and chemical ingredients we use in hundreds of products every day.

Stupp Corporation

Stupp Corporation, founded in 1952, is a world leader in the manufacture of custom steel line pipe. Located within eight miles of the largest tonnage volume inland deep water port in the United States, Stupp Corporation is a major supplier of pipelines to oil and gas companies around the world, and has had their pipe installed in lines as far away as Australia.

Located on more than 120 acres in North Baton Rouge, Stupp Corporation's facility is the most modern pipe manufacturing facility in the world. The company has the largest ERW pipe mill in North America and was the first ERW pipe mill in the world to produce 24-inch OD pipe. The company was also the first pipe producer to manufacture 64 foot and 84 foot pipe lengths and has been recognized both nationally and internationally for the quality of its American Petroleum Institute (API) Line Pipe. API sets the standard for pipe in the oil and gas industry.

In addition, Bayou Coating, L.L.C., the most modern pipe coating facility in North America, is located within the Stupp Corporation complex. Here, pipe coating, the last step in the manufacturing process, is done quickly with minimal travel and handling.

When Stupp Corporation first began operations, it was manufacturing invasion pipe for the American troops in the Korean Conflict. Throughout the decades, it has been dedicated to meeting the ever-changing needs of its customers and the market and has consistently demonstrated it can remain responsive to those demands.

In 1997, shortly after receiving extensive feedback from clients such as SONAT, Exxon, Transco, CIG, Enron, NOVA, and TransCanada, and analyzing future trends in the industry, Stupp Corporation installed a $30 million state-of-the-art pipe mill upgrade. The new technology has enabled the company to increase its capacity and flexibility, allowing it to respond to all segments of its markets. Most importantly, this upgrade has permitted the company to exceed its customer's expectations.

The facility upgrade introduced advanced technology in edge milling, cage forming, length optimization, new and faster beveling operations, video scanning of the ID scarf, and laser pipe measurements.

The most impressive addition in the upgrade is the company's accumulator. Housing the largest vertical accumulator in the world, Stupp Corporation can now manufacture more efficiently than operations utilizing a coil to coil operation. This cost-effective measure alone can save thousands of dollars for both Stupp Corporation and its customers.

However, while speed is impressive, it's not the only benefit. To understand why, one must understand the way things used to work.

In the old way of doing business, a process many pipe mills still depend on today, the mill was stopped every time the production process reached the end of a coil of steel. In order to continue manufacturing pipe, a new steel coil had to be carefully positioned back through the entire pipe forming process. This was similar to re-threading a needle and could be quite time consuming.

The accumulator, however, makes this step obsolete. There is now no need to thread the needle because with the accumulator, the lead end of one coil is attached to the back end of the previous coil, allowing a continuous ribbon of steel to form. This results in a continuous operation that not only increases the production of pipe, but it also ensures a higher level of quality for sustained periods.

For the energy industry, pipe to pipe consistency and quality is critical to a safe and cost effective energy infrastructure. That's why Stupp Corporation works diligently with its customers in achieving optimal safety and environmental standards. In fact, the company is keenly aware of these necessities especially after a gas company in Colorado, experienced certain events in the early 1990's.

Colorado Interstate Gas, CIG, used pipe manufactured at Stupp Corporation to complete a pipeline project that extended into parts of Wyoming, Colorado, and Utah. The

pipeline project also crossed through the land of the Ute Indian, often referred to as the "Blue Sky People." Here, the land is rugged country where hostile conditions are normal and phenomena of nature occur at random.

Shortly after the project was completed, CIG ran what is called a "cleaning pig" through the line to remove any accumulated liquid. When the cleaning pig arrived at the receiver, it was severely damaged. CIG then ran a geometry tool through to locate the section of the pipe causing the pig damage.

Once the section was found, the pipe was excavated. It showed severe buckles, yet despite the damage, the pipe was still in tact and operational. What could have been an environmental disaster was avoided. Investigators later determined the area had experienced some type of earth movement.

At Stupp Corporation, stories like this reflect the company's mission which is to manufacture superior products that improve quality of life and contribute to public and environmental safety. Every day, the company shows renewed commitment to its core values of honesty in work, integrity, safety, and professionalism.

Employees at Stupp Corporation are highly trained and experienced. The company's workforce has an average of over 20 years experience in pipe making, which plays a vital role in the success of Stupp Corporation. From 1992 to 1997, the Baton Rouge facility experienced an incredible safety record of over 1,700 days or 4 1/2 years without time lost to an accident.

A division of Stupp Bros., Inc., a family-owned company dating back five generations with holdings in such industries as gas distribution, structural steel fabrication, and banking, Stupp Corporation is committed to reinvesting in its workforce through continuous training. The company strongly believes these investments in people and equipment will provide a sustainable advantage in the marketplace, allowing it to better serve its customers, employees, and community.

Today, as it did in the past, the energy industry is continuously changing and looking for new resources. As market leaders appear to vigorously move toward deeper exploration offshore and into the tundra and jungle of other lands, Stupp Corporation will remain vigilant and determined to meet any new challenges that lay ahead. As a leader in its industry, Stupp Corporation, the energy filled company, is prepared and focused on providing the ultimate products and services to the energy market. ✣

Baton Rouge Coca-Cola Bottling Company

In all the annals of American business, there is probably no other product that can match the success story of Coca-Cola. Indeed, the Coca-Cola story is one firmly rooted in American entrepreneurship, and one of which the Baton Rouge Coca-Cola Bottling Company is proud to be a part.

First invented in the backyard of Atlanta pharmacist John S. Pemberton in 1886, Coca-Cola was touted simply as a "Delicious and Refreshing" drink. Interestingly, Pemberton used only the most basic of laboratory equipment to make his famous concoction including a brass kettle, percolator, measuring cups, ladles, and apothecary scales.

During its first year, Coca-Cola sales totaled 25 gallons, bringing in $50 of revenue with $46 of that amount going to advertising.

Over the years Coca-Cola's success has been phenomenal. Today, in 80 different languages, people all over the world ask for Coke more than a million times a day, and sales are well over the multi-billion dollar mark. Even vintage Coca-Cola ads and other nostalgic items have found renewed value in today's collectible market.

The Baton Rouge Coca-Cola Bottling Company has seen its own success mirror that of its parent company. Like the humble origins of the product itself, the Baton Rouge Coca-Cola Bottling Company began operations in 1906, and operated out of a one-story, barn-like building in the downtown area. The delivery system used was standard for the times, consisting of a wagon drawn by two mules.

During its first year of operation, the Baton Rouge Coca-Cola Bottling Company produced 196,000 bottles of Coke in the famous 6 1/2 oz. bottle.

Baton Rouge Coca-Cola Bottling Company remains privately owned after 93 years, but now operates as the Gulf Coast Region of Coca-Cola Bottling Company United, Inc. The company serves 23 parishes in Louisiana and 14 counties in Mississippi. Sales and distribution centers are located in Baton Rouge, Lake Charles, and Lafayette, Louisiana as well as in McComb, Gulfport, and Hattiesburg, Mississippi. All products for distribution are produced at the Baton Rouge and Hattiesburg plants.

"We have four state-of-the-art production lines constantly in use, producing 200 different product and package combinations for our company," said Gary Sligar, President of Gulf Coast Region, Coca-Cola Bottling Company United, Inc.

Over the years, the Baton Rouge plant has expanded its Coca-Cola brands to include Sprite, Surge, and Fruitopia, as well as other franchise brands such as Dr Pepper and Big Red. In addition, according to Sligar, non-carbonated brands are the fastest growing products with Minute Maid Juice, POWERaDE, Evian, and Laurel Mountain water leading the growth. "It is important that we have a taste for every thirst," said Sligar.

Through the years, the company has played a vital role in helping to make Baton Rouge not only a prosperous and growing city, but a city where family values and generosity still achieve success.

The company routinely helps underwrite many charitable and citywide events including Christmas on the River, Bonne Fete 300, and the Jaycees Christmas Parade. The company is also a major contributor to the Capital Area United Way, American Red Cross, Mary Bird Perkins Cancer Center, and virtually all other charities in the area that provide for the citizens of the Baton Rouge Community.

The Baton Rouge Coca-Cola Bottling Company also proudly supports education and youth sports. The company has provided scoreboards for practically every high school in the area, and continues to "partner" with every public and private school in the community. On the collegiate level, Coke is the official soft drink of Southern University and Louisiana State University.

"For nearly 100 years Coca-Cola and its unique taste has satisfied the thirst of Baton Rouge citizens, and we understand our corporate responsibility to give back to the consumers who have supported our company," said Sligar.

DEMCO

DEMCO began providing electricity in southeast Louisiana in 1938 and has progressed from a small predominantly rural cooperative with 781 member-customers to become a multi-million dollar corporation with over 72,000 member-customers in the parishes of Ascension, East Baton Rouge, East Feliciana, Livingston, St. Helena, Tangiaphoa, and West Feliciana.

Many factors have contributed to the success and growth of DEMCO during this past six decades. As utilities nationwide downsize and prepare for impending deregulation, DEMCO has continued to place emphasis on the one product it values the most: customer service.

How is this accomplished? DEMCO continuously updates and maintains its more than 7,600 miles of electric lines with state-of-the-art technology and equipment. By positioning itself as a leader in technology, the company not only continues to enjoy its competitive advantage as a business entity, but also increases its reliability as an electric utility to present customers.

Reliability, however, is not simply achieved by technology and equipment. Trained, knowledgeable employees also must be accessible to the customer. And at DEMCO, that is not a problem.

DEMCO mandates a comprehensive training program for its service technicians as well as continuing education and cross-training for other staff members. Cross-training helps ensure that the member-customers' concerns and questions are answered immediately. DEMCO also has another advantage when it comes to its employees.

Because it is a local company, most DEMCO employees live in the same parish where they work. They believe their job is a 24-hour commitment to their friends, family, and neighbors. For example, employees at DEMCO generously give back to their community by volunteering their time with such organizations as the United Way, Kiwanis, March of Dimes, and 4-H.

This same spirit of giving and community involvement also radiates from corporate officials. DEMCO management strongly believes in the education of today's youth. Each year, the cooperative sponsors four local high school juniors on a trip to Washington, D.C., to learn how the federal government operates. The company also awards, through a random drawing, full-time scholarships to public Louisiana universities, and employees donate their time to local schools as judges for school fairs and instructors for classes on electrical safety. In addition, employees also teach personal economics classes to students through Junior Achievement.

Education, of course, is not just for young people, and DEMCO is committed to encouraging others in the community to strive for higher personal and business goals. With this in mind, DEMCO created the Dixie Business Center (DBC). Through this project, entrepreneurs as well as existing small business owners gain knowledge and assistance in various areas from management and technical skills to venture capital and financial sources. The DBC also provides shared office space and services and recently added a new 23,000 square-foot building to house new businesses and manufacturing industries.

As DEMCO begins its seventh decade of providing electricity to homes and businesses in southeast Louisiana, the company is also strategically maneuvering its business plan to capture and create opportunities of growth.

DEMCO offers unique incentive rates to qualified businesses. These special rates also encourage community development and serve as a benefit to the entire area.

DEMCO is also interested in other avenues of growth, and the company, through its subsidiary, DEMCO Energy Services, Inc. (DESI), offers other services to the community. These include DEMCO.net for internet access; Strike Safe surge protection equipment; DEMCO Air, a joint venture to provide heating and air conditioning sales and service; and DESIcom of Louisiana, a 220 MHz voice and data communications system.

At first, some of these programs may catch the average customer by surprise. After all, why would an electric utility want to provide these other services?

To DEMCO, that answer is easy. Since its beginning, the company has always put the customer first. DEMCO believes by offering diverse products and services, the cooperative will not only meet additional needs of its member-customers, but will also become more efficient in the distribution of electricity. By becoming more efficient, DEMCO can continue its original mission of providing safe, reliable, and affordable electric power to the people of southeast Louisiana.

Associated Grocers, Inc.

Since its inception, Associated Grocers, Inc. has been dedicated to the survival and success of the independent retail grocer. Its professional staff is committed to the member-retailers and they strive to provide the highest quality products at the lowest possible cost, and the best retailer-focused services available.

This enables the members to:

- be competitive and aggressive in their respective marketing areas;
- have available new and innovative ideas for advertising, marketing, promotion, and technological services; and
- receive information on potential retail sites and assist in the evaluation of these sites as future locations.

"We are dedicated to the survival and success of our retailers, and feel the best way for our company and our member-retailers to succeed is to work together as a team," says J.H. Campbell, Jr., President and CEO of Associated Grocers, Inc. "This has been our philosophy of operation for the past 49 years, and we should continue to be successful in the future."

Associated Grocers, Inc. was organized on May 23, 1950 by 17 member stores. The original membership consisted of grocers from old and respected business families of Baton Rouge. From its humble beginnings in 1950, Associated Grocers, Inc. quickly developed into a success for Baton Rouge and eventually the southeastern region of the United States. The marketing strategy was simple, but effective. Through combined buying power, member-retailers decreased the cost of goods by purchasing directly from food manufacturers. The company began in a small 2,500 square foot warehouse located in downtown Baton Rouge near the Mississippi River, and over the past 50 years, it has grown and expanded, both in size and leadership.

In the past three years, the company expanded its warehouse and administrative facilities to include almost 600,000 square feet on Anselmo Lane. Membership has expanded to more than 230 retailers in Louisiana, Mississippi, and Texas. Under the leadership of current president J.H. Campbell, Jr., the company is on the leading edge of technology, offering its retailers a full line of services including accounting, advertising, engineering, marketing, retail technology, and merchandising.

With more than 550 full-time employees and annual sales of more than $400 million, Associated Grocers, Inc. is a key contributor to the economy of Louisiana and is the third largest privately held corporation in Baton Rouge.

Associated Grocers, Inc. will celebrate its 50th year of doing business in the year 2000. "Our founding philosophy is the reason we have been successful for the past 50 years," says Campbell. "By working together and trusting each other, every member-retailer knows that together they can be successful while still growing their own businesses separately."

"Diverse", "independent," and "hardworking" are words used frequently to describe the retail members of Associated Grocers, Inc. The term that describes them best is "entrepreneurial spirit." These retailers have dedicated their lives to serving the needs of their communities. As partners of Associated Grocers, Inc., more than 230 independent retail stores strive to succeed in the neighborhood marketplace by providing quality and service to their customers.

The retail members and employees of Associated Grocers, Inc. are also heavily involved with charitable and community organizations in the greater Baton Rouge area. Organizations such as the Greater Baton Rouge Food Bank, the American Heart Association, Louisiana Public Broadcasting, Bonne Fete 300, Mary Bird Perkins Cancer Center, the Louisiana Chapter of the Arthritis Foundation, Junior Achievement, and the Istrouma District of the Boy Scouts of America are all supported by Associated Grocers, Inc.

Associated Grocers, Inc. has taken a proactive approach to the issue of Year 2000 Compliance. Through the amazing teamwork and knowledge of the Information Services staff of Associated Grocers the Year 2000 Retail Readiness Kit was created. This kit was distributed to all member-retailers of Associated Grocers, Inc. to assist each retailer with Y2K compliance issues in their individual stores. The kit has been very effective in successfully assisting member-retailers of Associated Grocers with Y2K compliance and was sold and distributed by the National Grocers Association to retailers nationwide.

Associated Grocers, Inc. has also created a website, which gives the world a peek at the member-retailers and their distribution center. Internet users can access information about the history of the company, the different departmental services offered at the distribution center, as well as the nearest retail locations. "Over the past 50 years, we have accomplished our mission by adapting and changing decade to decade, year to year, and as needed, to the changing dynamics of the marketplace and the consumer," says J.H. Campbell, Jr. "That is what we must do to survive and to provide our member-retailers with the quality and services that they deserve." ✤

Profile submitted by Associated Grocers, Inc.

The Shaw Group Inc.

The Shaw Group Inc., headquartered in Baton Rouge, Louisiana, is a leading supplier of piping systems and a provider of industrial construction and maintenance services primarily for the electric power, chemical, petrochemical, refining, and oil and gas industries worldwide.

With facilities located throughout the United States as well as in several international countries, The Shaw Group is a world-leading innovator of turnkey piping systems. Most importantly, the Company is committed to being a "Total Piping Resource" for the energy industry, and has revolutionized the pipe fabrication industry by seamlessly integrating its comprehensive design and engineering services, piping system fabrication, manufacturing, and sale of specialty pipe fittings, design, and manufacture of pipe support systems and on-site installation.

In short, Shaw is integrating its companies to provide customers with the services they need from the beginning of a project to the end. Including access to its Company's highly trained engineering and design teams. Here, the Company capitalizes on its title as a recognized leader in state-of-the-art technology. For example, The Shaw Group's advanced plant design management software, such as ShawDraw and ShawMan, are directly linked to the Company's fabrication shops. This helps reduce lead times, lower total installed costs, and provide more comprehensive services for many of its industries' largest constructors as well as for a number of overseas projects.

Shaw houses the largest pipe fabrication capacity worldwide, and is a premier specialty pipe fittings manufacturer. The Company is also continuing to gain ground in its industry through various strategic acquisitions. These acquisitions include the 1998 purchase of Bagwell Brothers, Inc., a Louisiana-based offshore oil and gas fabrication and construction company, and Cojafex B.V., a Rotterdam, Holland company owning the most advanced technology for induction pipe bending.

On the leading edge of piping technology, Shaw owns the technology for induction pipe bending machines. The Baton Rouge-based company currently has eight induction-bending machines in operation, more than any other company in the world.

The Company's growth strategy has been two-fold. First, by occupying strong footholds in the marketplace, Shaw has become the lowest cost piping systems provider worldwide enabling the Company to provide results to customers not only in a timely manner, but in a more cost efficient manner as well.

Growth in diverse markets also positions the Company to effectively address changes in the marketplace, and better utilize its available resources.

"We are strategically situated to offer innovative solutions to new and existing customers in diverse industry segments and geographic locations. When new opportunities are presented, we will be better positioned to react and maximize the potential for increased profitability," said J.M. Bernhard, Jr., chairman, president and chief executive officer of The Shaw Group.

Bernhard founded the Company in 1987. Since going public in 1993 (the Company's common stock trades on the NYSE under the symbol SGR), The Shaw Group has consistently demonstrated strong sales and growth.

The above chemical plant in Louisiana is just one example of Shaw's integrated services and resource flexibility. As the general contractor on this extensive upgrade of an existing grass roots gas fractionation facility, Shaw administered the construction, provided the shop fabrication and fielded the installation of 2,500 pipe spools.

The Company's backlog continues to reach record levels, and at the end of the third quarter for fiscal year 1999, the Company reported backlog totaling approximately $781 million, a new high in Shaw's history.

Who are some of Shaw's customers? The Company's client list reads like an industry "Who's Who," including Exxon, Union Carbide, Shell, Albemarle, General Electric, and Westinghouse. In addition, Shaw has created an alliance partnership with several other industry leaders including ABB, Air Products, BASF, Dow Chemical, Orion, Alstom, Bayer, Bechtel, Dupont, Parsons, and Praxair.

The Shaw Group has facilities in California, Louisiana, New Hampshire, New Jersey, Oklahoma, South Carolina, Texas, Utah, Australia, the U.K., and Venezuela, as well as a joint-venture facility in Manama, Bahrain. Domestically and internationally, the Company employs more than 5,000 people. ✤

Georgia-Pacific

As one of the largest forest products companies in the world, Georgia-Pacific Group manufactures and distributes a wide range of wood and paper products, including building products, pulp, paper, and tissue. The company's Port Hudson Operations is located just north of Baton Rouge in Zachary, Louisiana. The local mill is a fine paper facility and employs more than 840 people, making it the seventh largest industry in the Baton Rouge area. The Georgia-Pacific Corporation board of directors approved construction of a new tissue-manufacturing machine at the Port Hudson Operations. The machine will support the group's rapidly growing consumer tissue business, which includes the brands Angel Soft®, Sparkle®, Coronet® and MD®. The approximately $90 million project, which is expected to be completed in 2001, will be capable of producing approximately 80,000 tons of premium tissue a year.

Georgia-Pacific's Port Hudson facility began operations in 1968. Since that time and continuing through today, the company has consistently acted upon its commitment of quality assurance and environmental stewardship by investing millions of dollars in facility renovations, safety training, and leading edge technology. In 1994, the company spent $31 million on a new chlorine dioxide generator that reduced elemental chlorine consumption. That same year, the firm also invested an additional $10 million to convert its paper making process from acid-based to alkaline-based resulting in longer lasting paper for consumers and reduced emissions for the environment.

Of course, Georgia-Pacific has implemented many other projects over the years to ensure success. From the installation of a $7.9 million Honeywell Measurex System (for consistent quality) to a $20 million upgrade on the company's paper machines and sheeter packaging line, each stage of the manufacturing process is designed to build product quality. The company uses state-of-the-art technology as well as onsite operators to achieve excellence in every product. This attention to detail is important, and it shows.

In 1997, Port Hudson received the Georgia-Pacific's Vice President's Quality Award. That same year, the facility also achieved a 100 percent Elemental Chlorine Free (ECF) bleaching operation and was named a Baton Rouge Green Award Winner. Other honors include the Chairman's Award for Environmental Excellence (1996) and the Chairman's Award for Most Improved OSHA Incidence Rate (1998).

The Port Hudson facility has also been noted for its commitment to safety, achieving OSHA's Voluntary Protection Program's (VPP) Star Site. The VPP is a nationally recognized program. The local facility was the second pulp and paper mill in the United States to be accepted into this program.

The company's philosophy of continuous improvement is also reflected in its efforts to serve its neighbors. While Georgia-Pacific selected the Port Hudson site because of its strategic location near both an abundance of natural resources and the nation's largest tonnage volume inland deep water port, the firm is very active in promoting environmental education and awareness. As such, the facility is very active in local schools, providing numerous financial and equipment donations as well as student scholarships. Active in the community of Greater Baton Rouge, Georgia-Pacific played an integral part in renovating the Old State Capitol Building. By contributing $100,000, the firm helped preserve a piece of Louisiana history.

Today, the company is focused on maintaining a piece of American history. The Port Hudson Civil War Battlefield, the site of the longest battle in United States military history, is located near the mill. In 1863, the Siege of Port Hudson by Federal Troops ultimately helped Federal Troops gain control over the Mississippi River, marking the beginning of the end to the Civil War. This historic battlefield, which is located on the firm's property, is being preserved thanks to Georgia-Pacific volunteers, the Port Hudson State Commemorative Park, and the Boy Scouts of America. It is one of the few Civil War battlefield sites remaining that is not owned by a state or federal government.

Through the years, the Port Hudson facility has supported the growth of other businesses in the area. The firm purchases $50 million of local goods and services per year and supports an annual payroll of $51 million. As a leader in the community, Georgia-Pacific continues to look to the future and will strive to maintain the high standard of quality and customer satisfaction it has developed. With its strong commitment to safety, the environment, and quality of production, the future of Georgia-Pacific is assured success in Baton Rouge. ✤

Photo by Philip Gould

Business and Finance

The Chamber of Greater Baton Rouge

Since 1920, The Chamber and its volunteer leadership have worked to represent the business community on issues that affect them. This commitment continues—stronger and more dedicated than ever—today and into the future.

Representing more than 1,500 companies with over 100,000 employees, the Chamber of Greater Baton Rouge works to accomplish for area businesses and the community at large what no individual or single business can do alone. The companies represented by the Chamber run the gamut from megacorporations to home-based businesses, from industrially driven manufacturers to the service and professional sectors. The Chamber's membership is as varied as the interests and concerns that impact the Greater Baton Rouge community every day.

With concern for the creation of new jobs, meeting the needs of new and existing business, and playing a lead role in economic and community development, the Chamber continues to develop programs that reflect new vision and quality leadership for the future, while providing valuable benefits to its membership.

Economic Development

Promoting and assisting economic development in the Greater Baton Rouge area is one of the major priorities of the Chamber. It is a key element in any community, and Baton Rouge is no different. We play a major role in attracting new business to the area, providing assistance to many new companies in the process of establishing operations, and addressing important issues on behalf of existing industry.

The Chamber has helped to forge many beneficial relationships between the business community and all levels of government to establish a "business-friendly" environment in Baton Rouge, a climate that fosters business growth and prosperity.

Chamber members have access to a wealth of economic information through the most comprehensive research library in the Baton Rouge area, providing them with unique insight into the growth of the Greater Baton Rouge economy. A large number of statistics are maintained on area demography, development, and business and are always available to Chamber members.

As a result of the region's continued growth, such factors as workforce development, transportation, planning, education, and new technology become even more critical to future development. The Chamber will put the best interests of the business community at the forefront as it addresses the issues that impact the economy.

Community Development

The Chamber plays a very important role in the area of community development. Issues pertaining to education, infrastructure, and the safety of area citizens all have a direct effect on economic development and the general quality of life in Baton Rouge. The Chamber deals with these issues every day in helping to keep Baton Rouge moving in the right direction.

The Chamber serves as a catalyst for positive community development, maintaining a close working relationship with local, state, and federal government, as well as key board and staff representation in many other area organizations dedicated to building a better Baton Rouge. The Chamber provides second-to-none leadership training for the future leaders of Baton Rouge and stays very involved with numerous key issues and initiatives that impact the community.

Through committee involvement and special briefings, members get the inside track on issues and a chance to actively participate in matters that affect their family, business, and community.

Member Services

Developing innovative, informative programs, and exposure opportunities for members has long been one of the Chamber's top priorities. From advertising opportunities on the Chamber website and in Chamber publications, to effective business educational programs, the Chamber provides and continues to develop a wide range of valuable benefits for its members.

Its organization offers a variety of ways that members can regularly interact with and benefit from other members of the Greater Baton Rouge business community. Participation in Chamber programs and involvement in Chamber committees and initiatives enables businesses to develop new business leads, expand their contacts in the community, and gain access to many helpful products and services.

The Chamber receives thousands of inquiries each year for products and services needed within the community, across the nation, and throughout the rest of the world. Individuals and firms making those inquiries are referred to Chamber members.

The Chamber provides a wide variety of valuable member services and strives to deliver the kind of benefits that provide a true competitive advantage to member businesses. It is constantly assessing the needs of its membership in order to develop the best possible programs, products, and services—the kind that have a positive impact on each business' bottom line.

Rapid economic growth brings with it significant opportunities and challenges. How a community deals with them directly affects the future of that community. Positive change and problem solving in a city the size of Baton Rouge does not happen by itself—it requires quality leadership, talent, and a strong dedication to getting things done.

The Chamber board and staff does not accomplish these things alone. The success of Baton Rouge's premier business organization is a direct result of the dedication and commitment of its membership.

Baton Rouge is moving in a positive direction. Regardless of what kind of technological, educational, financial, or environmental challenges the next century will bring, The Chamber will be there, helping to lead the way.

The Chamber's Mission

To provide leadership for the advancement of economic vitality and quality of life for its members and the total community. ✤

The Chamber plays an important role in representing local business interests to all levels of government. Taking strong positions on issues such as education, transportation, crime, economic, and community development that are in the best interest of our membership and community is a major function of the organization.

LUBA Workers' Compensation Fund

"By giving our clients more than they expect." That's how fund administrator David Bondy explains the success of Louisiana United Businesses Association Workers' Compensation Fund, the largest program of its kind in the state.

From cabinetmakers to retailers to contractors, the Fund is committed to helping every policyholder achieve and maintain excellent safety performance in their workplace, protect their employees from injury, and enhance their overall security and prosperity.

Louise Poupart of Poupart's Bakery, LUBA Policyholder.

Founded on the simple belief that Louisiana employers should have a choice among workers' compensation programs, the Fund was designed specifically to help small and medium-sized businesses in Louisiana obtain affordable workers' compensation coverage.

Since 1991, the LUBA Fund has been providing reliable, well-managed workers' compensation insurance at affordable rates. Endorsed by the Louisiana United Businesses Association (LUBA), a non-profit organization dedicated to the development and prosperity of Louisiana companies, the Fund also offers its policyholders the opportunity to earn large dividend returns. In the last five years, the Fund returned almost $8 million in unused premiums to its policyholders.

Debbie Lockhart, Marketing Coordinator, and David Bondy, C.E.O.

Today, the LUBA Fund is the plan of choice for thousands of Louisiana employers seeking a better alternative. The Fund has over $30 million in standard premiums in force and $769 million in insured payrolls.

When created, the LUBA Fund was an innovative solution to problems that had led to a dismal period in the state's insurance history. From 1980-1990, obtaining workers' compensation insurance in Louisiana was a nightmare. During that decade, factors such as rising medical costs, inflated insurance rates, mismanaged claims, inappropriate settlements, and fraud led to high rates and surcharges. In fact, at that time, many Louisiana companies experienced rate increases of more than 300 percent. Many national insurance companies abandoned the state, practically eliminating any choices for businesses.

Determined to provide a better alternative, the LUBA Fund was established to give Louisiana employers a choice. The Louisiana Department of Insurance approved the Fund effective January 21, 1991. The LUBA Fund collects premiums from member policyholders and then uses those assets to cover claims and to manage the Fund.

"Fundamentally, we are different (from other insurance carriers). Not only are we often less expensive up front, but by returning unused premiums to policyholders, many of our customers have actually cut their workers' comp cost in half," said Bondy. And for many Louisiana companies, the opportunity to receive big dividends at the end of the year is a great incentive for maintaining and encouraging a safe workplace.

"We've found that some of our business owners offer to share the company's dividend returns with employees at the end of the year. By offering the employees financial incentives for safety, there is often less downtime," added Bondy. "Productivity and morale is usually higher too."

An integral part of the LUBA Fund's success has been attracting and maintaining businesses that adhere to stringent safety programs. Consultants are on call statewide to advise companies in safety program development. Because the Fund insures a wide array of businesses, these consultants assist policyholders in a wide range of activities including customized training activities, OSHA assistance and state audits, and programs to achieve a drug-free workplace.

Clyde Roy, Senior Vice President, and Laurie Galbreath, Underwriter.

The Fund's comprehensive claims service pays claims rapidly and investigates suspected fraudulent claims quickly. Risk Management Services (RMS) is the service company providing underwriting, safety, and claims services. RMS is one of the state's largest service companies with offices in Baton Rouge and Metairie.

"If we owe a claim we pay it promptly, but if we suspect fraud we get tough," said Bondy. "We are a company that takes our responsibility seriously. We are firm and, most of all, fair."

The Fund's newest policyholder service is called *LUBA Care*. With a network of physicians and medical providers, *LUBA Care* is designed to provide specialized treatment in helping injured employees return to work faster.

"By creating *LUBA Care*, we have developed a network of physicians and medical providers who are focused on job-related injuries. With this kind of specialized care, the guesswork of an injury is eliminated and the worker can often recover and return to work quickly," explained Bondy. By choosing to invest time and money in its *LUBA Care* program, the Fund is demonstrating its caring attitude to both its policyholders and their employees.

Meeting the challenges of the future today is just one way LUBA honors its commitment to Louisiana business owners. By using state-of-the-art technology, the Fund provides fast access to claim files allowing members to get prompt responses to their information requests.

Yet, while technology serves an important purpose, LUBA is old-fashioned when it comes to providing superior customer service. That's one reason why the Fund still insists on having people, not a computer-generated message, answer the company's phones. Above all, the Fund is most proud of its reputation as a big company with a friendly, hometown personality.

By continuing its blend of affordable premiums and prompt personal service, the LUBA Workers' Compensation Fund is poised to provide Louisiana's employers a clear choice for many years to come. ⚜

Pictured from left to right: Michelle Marcello, Senior Claims Adjuster; Frances Meliet, Claims Adjuster; Ronnie Francis, Claims Manager; and Tami Lopushansky, Senior Claims Adjuster.

Baton Rouge Area Convention & Visitors Bureau

As in any city, tourism is big business in Baton Rouge. The economic impact from tourism accounts for almost one billion dollars a year in the Capital City, and one reason why Baton Rouge is so successful in attracting visitors is because of the Baton Rouge Area Convention & Visitors Bureau.

As the official marketing arm of the city, the Bureau is entrusted with selling Baton Rouge to regional, national, and international markets. Day after day, the Bureau aggressively promotes Baton Rouge as the destination of choice for group, business, family, and individual travelers.

"What draws visitors to Baton Rouge is the people, history, and our way of life here. Baton Rouge is unique in that everywhere you turn, you experience a different part of Louisiana," says Leon Maisel, president and CEO of the Baton Rouge Convention & Visitors Bureau.

Since its charter in 1972, the Bureau has consistently worked to improve the city's economy and create more local jobs by increasing the number of visitors to Baton Rouge. Indeed, the Bureau's advertising campaign, which markets Baton Rouge as "Authentic Louisiana at Every Turn," has achieved that mission. By capitalizing on the area's own engaging history and culture, the Bureau has successfully positioned Baton Rouge as *the place* to be to see all that Louisiana has to offer. From Old South plantations and swamp tours, to live music and the state's world-famous cajun and creole food, the Bureau has found that location is most important, and that visitors like to be in the middle of all that makes Louisiana special. Only Baton Rouge can offer that excitement.

The Bureau is supported largely by a four percent lodging tax collected through all East Baton Rouge Parish hotels/motels. This solid economic base allows the Bureau to market Baton Rouge and compete aggressively with other cities for the lucrative tourism dollar. Economic impact statistics prove that local taxpayers receive a strong return on their investment. In 1997, the latest year statistics were available, East Baton Rouge Parish received $196.17 in direct tourism revenue from every dollar spent by the Bureau.

During that same year, the Bureau also achieved its most successful year yet. Bureau bookings alone were responsible for a $38 million economic impact to the city of Baton Rouge. These bookings included several major sporting events, national military reunions, business meetings, and tour groups.

Despite those impressive numbers, however, the Bureau insists it is only scratching the surface. The city can attract more visitors, and voters apparently agree.

In November of 1998, voters in East Baton Rouge Parish agreed to approve funding for expansion of the city's convention center, the Centroplex. The expansion will include 100,000 square feet of contiguous exhibition space and an additional 35,000 square feet of meeting space. The expansion is expected to make Baton Rouge a premier second-tier destination city for meetings and conventions, and will allow the Bureau to take advantage of a growing trend in groups wanting to use more economical and "user friendly" cities like Baton Rouge.

A recent study conducted by KPMG Peat Marwick shows that the market for groups desiring 100,000 square feet has grown from five percent to over 12 percent of the total market. By expanding the Centroplex, Baton Rouge will enjoy an economic impact of more than $17.9 million per year in direct spending and $1.5 million per year in projected tax revenues, according to the study.

This growing market and the opportunity the expansion brings to the city is enabling the Bureau to sell Baton Rouge at a much faster pace than ever before realized. Through direct sales efforts, advertising campaigns, and public relations, the Bureau, which is guided by a 10-member commission, is showing that Bureau is steadfastly proving that Baton Rouge is the *real* Louisiana. ✤

Washer, Hill & Lipscomb

Capitalizing on more than 20 years of extensive industry-wide experience, Washer, Hill & Lipscomb, An Architectural Corporation, has emerged as one of the most prominent full-service architectural firms in the Capitol City.

The firm's three principle partners, Russell Washer, Michael Hill and Richard Lipscomb, have combined their creative and technical talents with a team of highly skilled and seasoned employees. Together they have demonstrated, project after project, how to meet complex challenges while maintaining high quality of design.

The firm's work speaks for itself. Included in its portfolio are several projects which have received not only local but also national recognition. From the LSU Lod Cook Alumni Center and Hotel Complex to the Baton Rouge General Health Center and Health Center Campus Development, each project illustrates Washer, Hill & Lipscomb's broad range of high quality architectural experience.

But the ability to bring sophisticated solutions to design challenges and opportunities is only one aspect of this award winning firm. The Architectural Corporation prides itself on maintaining long-standing successful relationships with its many clients. In fact, many of its large corporate clients continue to call upon Washer, Hill & Lipscomb year after year. It's a vote of confidence the firm takes seriously.

Indeed, it is this type of reputation that not only guarantees quality, but also ensures trust. At Washer, Hill & Lipscomb, architecture grows from a rich heritage of shared community traditions and conventions; history that is then reinterpreted to reflect the present while at the same time project toward the future.

For the professionals at Washer, Hill & Lipscomb, architecture is more than just a blueprint. They know the buildings we live and work in affect our health, our job performance, our leisure, even our very thoughts and emotions. So, if our buildings work well, then our community, culture, hence, even our very lives will be enhanced. It is a design approach that has established and continues to bring success to the Baton Rouge-based firm.

Selected by the A.I.A. Academy of Architecture for health as an outstanding design, the Baton Rouge General Health Center integrates the highly technical aspects of modern medicine in a patient friendly environment.

The Lod Cook Alumni Center at LSU serves as a gathering point for alumni from all over the world, and is the winner of an A.I.A. Baton Rouge Rose Award for Design Excellence.

Fine quality custom residential design has been a hallmark of Washer, Hill & Lipscomb since the firm's inception.

Adams and Reese LLP

Adams and Reese is entrepreneurial, innovative and creative," says Eddy Quijano, managing partner of the law firm of Adams and Reese LLP, and manager of the firm's Baton Rouge office. "These words symbolize who we are."

1996 Halloween Big Buddy Party. Teresa Kalwoda, an Adams and Reese employee, has been the witch since 1990.

Certainly, for most people, words such as "entrepreneurial, innovative, and creative" are not typically associated with lawyers and the law profession, but then again, Adams and Reese is not your typical law firm.

Founded in New Orleans, Louisiana in 1951, Adams and Reese is a virtual legal powerhouse with offices in six key cities across the region, including Baton Rouge; Jackson, Mississippi; Houston, Texas; Mobile, Alabama; and Washington, D.C. The firm was one of the first in the area to recognize that business and legal issues in the dynamic region of the Gulf South are regional in nature and demand regional solutions.

Throughout the past decades, the firm's experience, skills, and resources have established it as THE law firm for today's Gulf South. In addition, Adams and Reese's strategic locations and civil code experience also make it a natural choice for businesses seeking a gateway to Mexico and Central and South America.

Adams and Reese employs more than 175 attorneys and has a combined staff of over 470 men and women to help meet the needs of its clients. In the last 20 years, it has tripled in size. As a large regional law firm, Adams and Reese specializes in a wide array of practice areas including Antitrust and Trade Regulation, Bankruptcy, Gaming, Intellectual Property, Oil and Gas, Products Liability, and Tax.

The firm first opened an office in Baton Rouge in 1984. It was the first office the firm opened outside of New Orleans, and back then, it was easy to see why Baton Rouge was chosen. Adams and Reese simply had one goal in mind: to provide better service to clients with interests in the Capital City.

As client service became more efficient, so did the firm's creative and innovative style. One aspect of that can be seen today in the firm's ability to become seamlessly integrated. This is accomplished through sophisticated communications systems and technical support. These avenues allow lawyers and staff at different offices to share resources and work together resulting in coordinated business and legal strategies for every client.

Another example of Adam and Reese's innovative style can be seen in the firm's management. Always able to "think out of the box," the firm has definitely benefited from a progressive style of management.

"We recognize that we were trained as lawyers, not as business people," says Quijano. That's why the firm regularly conducts management and leadership workshops for its partners, including a program LSU specifically designed for the firm. While this is a unique concept for many professional firms, Adams and Reese has found that continuing education and training opportunities helps employees develop a clearer vision of the firm's long-term and short-term goals. In turn, they are better able to provide more efficient and higher quality services while at the same time building trust, mutual respect, and long-term relationships with clients.

But this progressive style of management has other implications as well. Adams and Reese has long recognized the importance of community and civic involvement. Through the firm's own non-profit program called HUGS (Hope, Understanding, Giving, Support), lawyers and staff throughout the region participate in more than 30 community service activities.

"Our commitment to civil and charitable service is an essential part of our culture," says Quijano. "Our firm provides separate funding and resources so HUGS can continue to help those in need."

The firm's enthusiasm for service is matched only by the many awards it has received. Among the most notable include the 1993 Award for Excellence in Corporate Community Service given by the national Points of Light Foundation in Washington D.C., and the 1995 Excellence in Corporate Volunteerism Award presented by Volunteer BatonRouge!

Other organizations recognizing Adams and Reese include the Louisiana Association of Retarded Citizens, the American Red Cross—Louisiana Capital Chapter, and the East Baton Rouge Parish School Board. In addition, several lawyers and staff members have also been honored for their own individual contributions to various charitable organizations in Baton Rouge.

"We opened our office in Baton Rouge with one lawyer and one secretary from New Orleans. We now have over 50 people just here in Baton Rouge, and our vision is to continue to grow, and to continue to share our time and talents with the community," says Quijano. ✦

1995 Fix up at Prescott Middle School.

IBM

IBM was incorporated in 1911 as the Computer-Tabulating-Recording Co. with a product line that included time clocks, scales, and punch card tabulators. Today, IBM is the world's leading information technology company creating, developing, and manufacturing the industry's most advanced computer systems, software, networking systems, storage devices, and microelectronics.

IBM prides itself on helping customers apply those technologies to improve what they do and how they do it. IBM's professionals provide expertise within specific industries, consulting services, systems integration, solution development, and technical support.

IBM is also committed to and uniquely suited to addressing e-business opportunities, needs, and challenges by helping customers take advantage of the power of the Internet by becoming Web-enabled.

"Every day it becomes more clear that the Net is taking its place along side the other great transformational technologies that first challenged, then fundamentally changed, the way things are done in the world," says Lou Gerstner, Chairman and CEO of IBM.

"Certainly the Net is a powerful medium for communication. But even more important, it is a vocational medium—a place where real work gets done, real competitive advantage is gained, and real growth is generated," he adds.

Indeed, that outlook has been the driving force behind the success of IBM's Baton Rouge office. Through the last decades, the company has played a vital role in helping other businesses and government entities grow and prosper in the Capital City.

From providing the technology so businesses can process large volumes of information, such as payroll, to enhancing classroom instruction in student labs, to helping state agencies increase their efficiency and better serve citizens, IBM has made it their business to find solutions that work for any information technology problem.

At IBM, industry specific solutions are found daily. Client executives trained in the problems and strengths of an industry work exclusively with businesses in that field. IBM Client Executives use their knowledge, experience, and access to the company's world-renowned research division to create solutions that in many cases are not just industry specific, but are also first-of-a-kind projects for customers.

For example, in 1998, for the sixth consecutive year, the U.S. Patent and Trademark Office awarded IBM more new patents than any other company. IBM received 2,658 patents that year. Many were used to solve specific solutions for customers.

Certainly, that's why some of the largest and most profitable businesses in Louisiana as well as several government agencies have chosen IBM's advanced information technologies to solve their information technology problems. But there is also another reason why these businesses and government entities have chosen IBM.

As a leader in its industry, IBM recognizes the need for continuous support and training. For many, the hard work involved in implementing a technological solution can seem overwhelming, but IBM takes great pride in making the complicated look simple, and in heading off problems before anyone even knows about them.

The IBM Building located at Sherwood Forest and I-12.

That is especially important for government customers because how governments rethink and redesign their service delivery processes using technology will affect their future growth and competitiveness.

"IBM's objective is to enable governments to deliver better, faster, higher quality services to citizens in new ways through the innovative application of technology, including the Internet," says James Driesse, a local client executive and IBM's senior state executive for Louisiana.

Other groups also look to IBM for help, and the more than 84 employees at the company's Baton Rouge office are always ready to lend a hand. From supporting The United Way to working with Baton Rouge Green and picking up litter, there is a strong sense of social responsibility present.

One of the most important and most enjoyable way for these IBM employees to give back to their community is through education. Hardware and software are given annually to select schools so that every child can experience the wonder of technology and learn to live in a society that, like IBM, has embraced this fast-paced computer industry. ✤

Jim Driesse, IBM's Senior State Executive, (second from right) assembles his sales and marketing team in the State Capitol's Senate Chamber.

Diverse Funding Associates, LLC

Donald White, founder and executive consultant of Diverse Funding Associates, LLC, is confident about the future of his firm in Baton Rouge and believes strongly in giving back to the community. He is a regular contributor and member of several civic and charitable organizations in the area including 100 Black Men. Photo by Shane Johnson

The backbone of any successfully growing city is small businesses, and Baton Rouge is no exception. Since 1997, Diverse Funding Associates, LLC, a participant in one of the fastest growing sectors of the financial industry, has been helping the area's thriving small business community stay strong and competitive.

"We specialize in helping young businesses, or any business that is struggling," said Donald White, executive consultant and founder of Diverse Funding.

"Our services also extend to individuals and larger companies, basically we can help anyone that has created a note and is expecting money in the future," added White.

As a member of the American Cash Flow Association, a vast nationwide network providing access to billions of dollars in funding sources, Diverse Funding acts as a vehicle in the lucrative financial secondary market buying, selling, and brokering notes—such as an invoice or an "IOU."

"Let's say you own a business and it's struggling. Either you can't or don't want to get a bank loan, yet you are sitting on invoices or money owed to you (such as a 30-60-90 day note)," said White.

"Would it be more valuable to you to pay a percentage to a funding source so that you can receive this money now and buy more inventory, or would you want to take the cash and pay off a prior loan, helping to reduce your interest rates?" White asked.

"Or would you prefer to use the money to expand your business and increase your revenue?"

For many small business owners in Baton Rouge, the answers to these questions have been a resounding "yes." Since its inception, Diverse Funding has helped hundreds of businesses in the area remain profitable, keeping the city's robust marketplace alive and healthy.

Diverse Funding specializes in providing services to individuals. This includes buying and selling notes or so-called income streams, such as letters of credit, state lottery winnings, royalties, and court-awarded structured settlements.

"We are not actually lending money," said White. "Instead, our industry uses the time value of money which tells us that money is worth less in the future."

White explained that when an individual or business sells an income stream and accepts a lesser amount than the total amount due in the future, that person or company is actually saving money in the long run—especially if they choose to invest the cash.

At Diverse Funding, offering individuals and businesses various financial options is important. The firm is committed to meeting the individualized needs of each client and can assist with any transaction in the cash flow industry, including real estate.

"As Diversified Cash Flow Specialists, our firm's consultants are high-skilled and knowledgeable. We give the personal attention needed so businesses and individuals can make the best decision for their financial future," said White. ✦

Discussing future strategies in the fast-growing Cash Flow Industry are several consultants and executive consultants with Diverse Funding Associates, LLC: Judy Auzenne, Murphy Auzeene, Jr., Steacylea White, and Donald White, the firm's founder. Photo by Shane Johnson

Photo by Philip Gould

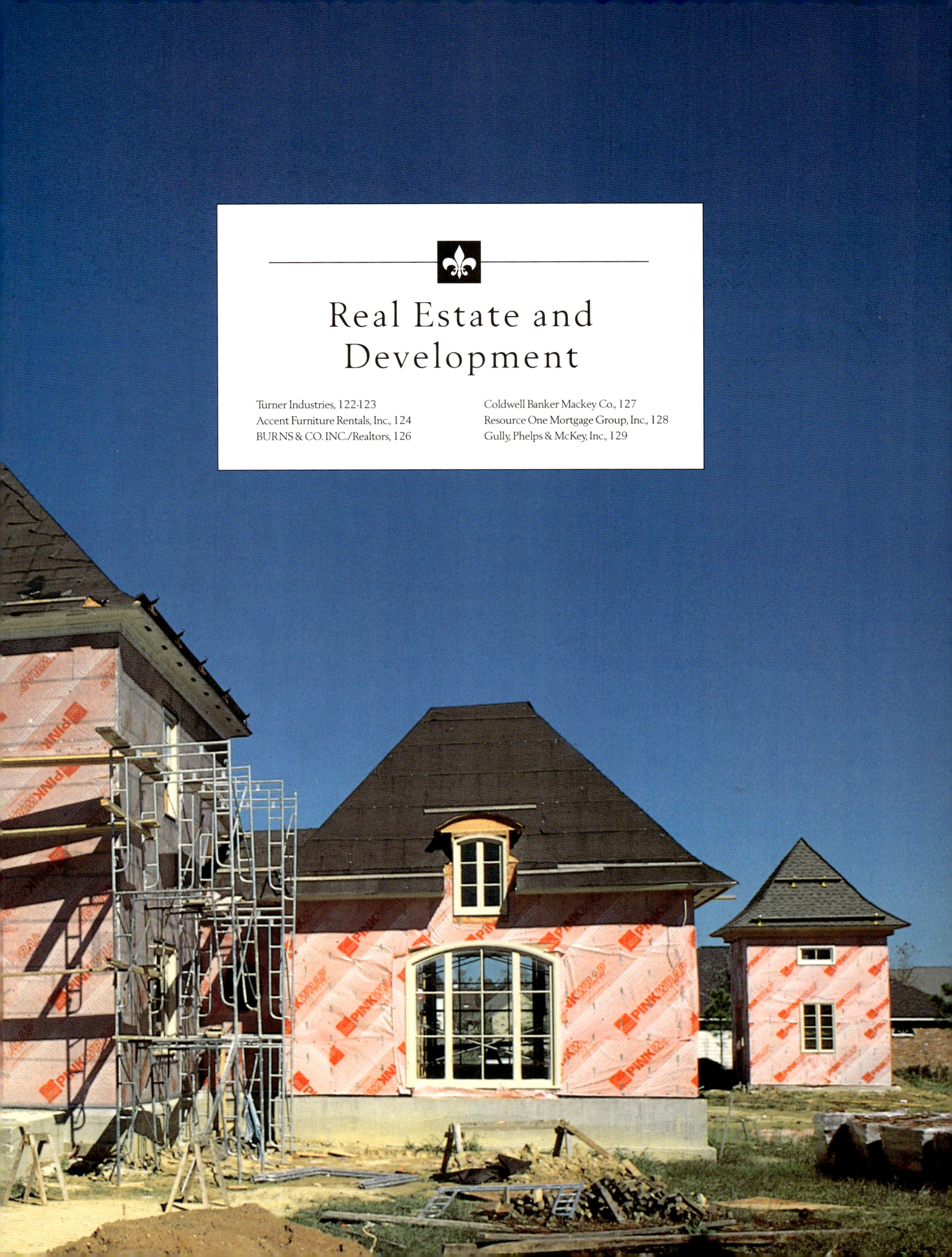

Real Estate and Development

Turner Industries

Seated: Bert S. Turner, Turner Industries Chairman of the Board. From Left: Thomas H. Turner, Turner Industries Executive Vice President, Roland M. Toups, Turner Industries President, J.W. Guitreaux, International Maintenance Corporation President, Don L. McCollister, Harmony President, and David R. Carpenter, Turner Industries Chief Financial Officer.

A nationally recognized leader in industrial services for more than three decades, Turner Industries, LTD. (TIL) is a group of diversified companies providing the necessary services to complete industrial projects for clients world wide. Based in Baton Rouge, Louisiana the firm is one of the largest privately owned industrial contractors in the United States, reporting sustained growth and annual sales of more than $700 million.

TIL is comprised of a family of 15 subsidiary companies with regional offices in Louisiana, Texas, and Alabama. Each company in the TIL family was created to meet specific client needs: including construction, contract maintenance, turnarounds, equipment rental, heavy hauling and rigging, pipe bending and fabrication, scaffold rental and erection, environmental services, non-destructive testing, predictive maintenance, bundle pulling, vacuum services, tank lifting and repair, employee leasing, information technology services, and temporary placement. The firm is a full service contractor and has contracts that extend across the United States from California to Delaware and international operations from South America to Eastern Europe.

With more than 5,000 workers locally, TIL is one of the largest employers in East Baton Rouge Parish. The firm has a combined total work force of more than 10,000 people, and through its 75,000-person database, is able to provide a total "job-ready" work force for any project.

Founded in 1962, TIL has built a solid reputation based on hard work, performance, and solid management. Under the leadership of founder and chairman, Bert S. Turner, TIL continues to maintain the highest standards of quality and safety in the industrial construction industry.

TIL traces its history back to Nichols Construction Company, which was incorporated in 1957. Turner joined this small but growing industrial construction firm leaving the security of a management position with Esso (the predecessor to Exxon). For the next 15 months, Turner worked as an assistant to Bob Nichols, the firm's founder and owner. When Nichols died unexpectedly, Turner was asked to run the company, which he did until it was sold to California-based Yuba Consolidated Industries.

Despite his own aspirations of business ownership, Turner chose to stay on board at Yuba. With Turner at the helm, the Nichols division did well, but parent company Yuba began experiencing financial troubles, eventually filing bankruptcy. It was during this process that Turner acquired the local construction company and much of its equipment out of bankruptcy proceedings.

As principal owner and president of the new Nichols, Turner and the firm continued to specialize in industrial construction securing jobs with many of the large petroleum and chemical plants from Baton Rouge to New Orleans. Initially, the company concentrated on repair and renovation, then added construction capabilities throughout the Gulf Coast.

Today, Nichols Construction Corporation, which specializes in heavy equipment, hauling, and rental is just one of 15 companies under the operating arm of TIL. Turner first began spinning off companies from Nichols in 1963. Ultimately, the unique structure of TIL gives the firm more control of all elements of a construction job, helping to secure its position in the market.

In addition to Nichols Construction Corporation, other subsidiaries in TIL's family of companies include National Maintenance Corporation (NMC) and International Maintenance Corporation (IMC). Both companies were created to serve as maintenance contractors to plants, independent of the construction end of the business.

In the early 1970s, Harmony Corporation was started. As an open shop industrial general contractor providing both construction and maintenance services, Harmony is one of TIL's top revenue producing divisions. In 1990,

Aerial shot of the 105 acre facility of Turner International Piping Systems in Paris, Texas. This company specializes in pipe fabrication, bending, and coatings.

Nichols Construction Corporation supplied their 800 ton and 200 ton Truck Cranes to lift the Space Shuttle Enterprise on its way to the 1984 World's Fair in New Orleans.

1994, 1995, 1996, and 1998 Harmony won the National Associated Building Contractor 's Award for "Excellence in Construction."

Shortly after Harmony was started, Industrial Technical Company (ITC) was created to provide non-destructive testing and predictive maintenance services. ITC has been instrumental in helping TIL secure additional jobs in plants where the firm's subsidiaries operate, as well as in non-contract operations.

Over the years, several other companies have been acquired or created by TIL. In the late 1970s, Crest Incorporated, a Beaumont, Texas-based company, was acquired complete with a steel fabrication shop to supplement TIL's industrial construction operations in the Beaumont, Port Arthur, and the Orange, Texas, areas.

Scafco Limited, a scaffold erection, rental, and sales operation supports TIL's construction and maintenance activities as does Integrated Technical Services Incorporated (ITS), an environmental services and asbestos abatement firm. In addition, Turner Industrial Services (TIS) provides clients with contract maintenance, heat exchanger maintenance, and bundle extraction, and Turner Corporation serves as a turnaround specialist, tank lifting, and bottom repair firm in plants where TIL has no existing contracts.

International Painting Corporation (IPC) services client needs in industrial painting. Using a climate-controlled facility, the environmentally sound procedure, includes abrasive blasting and protective coatings for fabricated and straight run pipe, steel, vessels, and equipment.

TIL also meets the industry's demand for cost effective pipe fabrication and bending services. International Piping Systems Limited (IPS) is a world leader in pipe and structural bending. Located in Port Allen, Louisiana, with direct access to the Intracoastal Waterway, IPS uses a state-of-the-art 200,000 square foot facility to serve clients in the pipeline, power, petrochemical, refinery, and paper industries. TIL's pipe fabrication capabilities were further expanded in 1999 with the acquisition of a 350,000 square foot shop in Paris, Texas.

Rounding out the list of TIL's family of companies is Turner Professional Services. As a professional employer organization, Turner Professional Services performs extensive pre-employment screening and testing and has regionally located recruiting offices and specialized multi-training facilities.

At TIL, there is a total commitment to quality and safety. The firm provides comprehensive safety training and has received numerous safety awards including the National Business Roundtable Industry Safety Award and the Associated Maintenance Contractors' Annual Award for Safety. Not surprisingly, safety performance statistics at TIL exceed industry standards.

In addition to job performance, the firm is commitmented to the community. TIL takes its job as a corporate citizen seriously and makes regular charitable contributions as well as supporting both corporate and employee involvement in civic and charitable organizations throughout the Baton Rouge area.

TIL prides itself as being the largest privately owned industrial construction and maintenance organization in the State of Louisiana. Engineering News Record in 1998 ranked TIL the No. 1 Industrial Maintenance Contractor in the United States, quite an accomplishment for that small financially troubled firm acquired by Bert S. Turner in the early 1960's. ✤

Harmony Construction Project in Geismar, Louisiana for Air Products and Chemicals. Harmony was awarded the 1998 National Associated Builders and Contractors Award for this DNT Facility.

Accent Furniture Rentals, Inc.

Strong family-owned businesses are the backbone of every thriving city. In Baton Rouge, Accent Furniture Rentals, Inc. is a fine example of a successful local business conveniently located on Florida Boulevard and blessed with dedicated employees, Accent has experienced phenomenal growth since its founding by the Warren family 22 years ago.

Left to Right; Mary Craig Warren, Robert Warren, Malloy Warren, and Malloy Warren Ryan.

From its beginnings in an unheated warehouse, Accent has grown to be Baton Rouge's premier furniture rental company and indeed, Louisiana's largest home-owned full-service furniture rental company. Owners Bob and Malloy Warren point with pride to the fact that they are a Louisiana enterprise, "contributing exclusively to our own state's economy."

The Warrens credit their excellent staff for much of their ongoing success.

"We are so lucky to have such a wonderful group of dedicated and knowledgeable employees, some of whom have been with Accent for over 15 years," Malloy Warren says. "Such a stability and consistency is rare among businesses today."

The key word at Accent is service.

"We try hard to treat each customer in a special way and to be as accommodating as possible with satisfaction guaranteed," says Malloy Warren.

"The person who needs rental furniture is often in the process of moving and is short of time. We try to be understanding and flexible—that's the beauty of a local company."

"Selecting our own furniture is another advantage," she adds. "From the beginning I've felt strongly that there is no reason that rental furniture can't be beautiful. I enjoy going to market and I select each piece with great care, from residential to office furniture."

A major part of Accent's market is its office furniture. Many lines of name brand office furniture including desks, credenzas, chairs, bookcases, tables, and waiting room furniture are available.

Another service offered at Accent is the "Corporate Apartment." For several years, this has been an important part of Accent's menu of services. A business person in town for a temporary assignment can enjoy the comfort and convenience of an attractive, furnished apartment rather than a lengthy hotel stay.

"We can arrange for an apartment, condominium, or house complete with furniture, appliances, electronics, linens, kitchenware, utilities, cable, and maid service. We've had an excellent response from businesses who want to offer this service to their employees."

Model homes are another of Accent's special services. The staff at Accent places accessories, pictures, and lamps as well as furniture in a model home. A furnished model enhances the appeal of the home to the public.

Accent's retail sales have increased in response to a booming economy. "We are frequently asked to design medical lobbies or doctor's offices. Our designer works with customers to choose fabrics and designs that give each room a special look."

A new Clearance Center on Goodwood Boulevard provides a large selection of pre-rented residential and office furniture, offering quality furnishings at greatly reduced prices.

"In fact, our services are quite broad. In addition to furniture and accessories, we rent and sell linens and kitchenware, offer free decorating services to our customers, and find temporary housing for people new to the area," says owner Malloy Warren.

A visit to Accent Furniture Rentals is a special treat. You'll discover a showroom full of tasteful furnishings and a genuine warm welcome. ✤

Left to Right; Jean Fritchie, Laura Mello, Stephanie Mouhot, Sandy Anderson, Melisa Lavender, and Dundie Frideley.

Photo by Philip Gould

BURNS & CO. INC./Realtors

BURNS & CO. INC/Realtors Country Club of Louisiana office location.

Bringing together over 200 years of combined real estate experience, BURNS & CO. INC/Realtors is committed to continuing its tradition of real estate excellence in the Baton Rouge area. From assisting homebuyers in entering the real estate market for the first time to handling some of the area's landmark properties, BURNS & CO. has consistently provided personalized and professional real estate services to its customers and clients.

"Our commitment to the industry is evident in the many advanced designations held by our associates. We have achieved expert status in our field by earning such advanced designations as the Graduate Realtors Institute (GRI), Certified Residential Specialist (CRS), Certified Real Estate Brokerage Manager (CRB), and Certified Relocation Specialist (CRS)," said Paul Burns, president of the firm.

Since the company was founded in 1993, BURNS & CO. has experienced tremendous growth. Of course, some of that growth is attributed to the city's busy real estate market, but the majority of the firm's success lies within the type of real estate professional consistently recruited and attracted to the firm. At BURNS & CO., experience, effort, and excellence are desired. As a result, most associates with the firm continuously reach personal real estate sales of more than a million dollars a year, achieving one of the industry's highest honors time and time again.

BURNS & CO. is also an innovator in exploring new ways to better serve the firm's customers and clients. In fact, the firm's diversified services have enabled it to be the provider of brokerage service for fine homes located in neighborhoods such as Bocage, Jefferson Place, Country Club of Louisiana, Pikes Lane, Lakeshore, and many others.

Recognizing the need to provide concrete solutions in today's ever-changing industry, BURNS & CO. is a member of RELO Relocation Network, the world's premier referral network.

As an affiliate of this industry network leader, BURNS & CO. is in a unique position to help families relocating in or out of the Baton Rouge area. The firm's relocation division offers a wide array of services including orientation area tours, group moves, newcomer packets, individual counseling, and other services needed to enhance a smooth move for the transferee.

BURNS & CO. can also assist families moving to another country. Whether an international move is by choice or company transfer, BURNS & CO. has the information to help families plan every aspect of their move from homefinding assistance to learning about the new country's customs, culture, and practices.

BURNS & CO. has offices at the Country Club of Louisiana and at Jefferson Highway, at Wrenwood. Associates are active in the local, state, and national associations of realtors. Their commitment to the community is illustrated by their strong involvement in such organizations as the Baton Rouge Chamber of Commerce, Community Fund for the Arts, Arts Council of Baton Rouge, Battered Women's Program, Baton Rouge Little

Paul R. Burns, President and Linda M. Dowden, Secretary/Treasurer.

Theatre, Baton Rouge Symphony, the Rotary Club of Baton Rouge, Junior League of Baton Rouge, and many other civic organizations.

"As individuals we are committed to the continual growth of our community and the need for every citizen to be involved. As a company, we are committed to providing quality service and experience. We believe our commitment and strength is a collective spirit, effort, and ethics of our associates and staff," Burns said.

Coldwell Banker Mackey Co.

Marge Mackey is, quite literally, sold on Baton Rouge.

As the owner of Coldwell Banker Mackey Company, REALTORS, the largest locally owned and operated real estate brokerage firm in the Greater Baton Rouge Metropolitan area, Mackey anticipates more growth for the Capitol City and has positioned her company to remain a leader in the local real estate market.

"Baton Rouge has so much to offer. This is a wonderful, family-oriented community with good industry, a good economy, a good political climate, and two major universities (Louisiana State University and Southern University)," said Mackey, founder and chairman of the board for Coldwell Banker Mackey Co.

A long-time veteran of the local real estate market, Mackey has received many honors and has consistently ranked in the top 10 of Residential Sales for the last 28 years with over 1,500 transactions and $150 million in sales production.

"Baton Rouge also has a spirit. I think it's that Cajun spirit, and it's catchy. I came here many decades ago from two feet of snow. All I had to do was put my feet on the ground to say I was staying," she added.

Mackey founded Coldwell Banker Mackey in 1975. At that time, the company was called The Mackey Company, REALTORS, and operated from a single small office with three sales agents and a secretary. Several years later, the firm became affiliated with Coldwell Banker, one of the largest and most respected full service real estate companies in the country, providing worldwide corporate employee relocation services. For more than 90 years the COLDWELL BANKER organization has been the country's premier full service provider of real estate services.

Today, Coldwell Banker Mackey has three offices in the Baton Rouge area with more than 90 associates and support staff. The firm's main office is located in a two-story building on South Sherwood Forest Boulevard, the so-called nerve center of the local real estate industry. From its company-owned 10,000 square foot building, the firm's corporate, commercial, relocation, property management, and one residential branch office are operated.

The firm's other full service brokerage offices are located in two of the fastest growing areas of the metroplex: Ascension Parish on Airline Highway and Highland Road, one mile west of I-10.

Through the years, Coldwell Banker Mackey has achieved success by providing quality and caring real estate services. The firm's sales associates maintain the highest level of professional integrity and ethics. Each agent has a thorough knowledge in real estate and local market trends and is extensively trained in the use of technology and the key role it now plays in the real estate industry.

As it did when it was founded, Coldwell Banker Mackey remains committed to providing buyers and sellers with the highest quality and most appropriate tools needed to make wise real estate decisions. Whether it's helping a young family move into their first home, or assisting a large corporation in relocating valued employees, the firm takes great pride in helping people make these important decisions. At Coldwell Banker Mackey Co., that's the best reason for doing business in Baton Rouge. ⚜

Coldwell Banker Mackey Co. positioned for the future.

Marge Mackey, founder and chairman of the board for Coldwell Banker Mackey Co.

Resource One Mortgage Group, Inc.

When Bill Walker named his mortgage company Resource One only two years ago, he had no idea how significant the word 'one' would be for the young company. In just a few short years, Walker has led the firm to become the number one mortgage company in the market.

Based in Baton Rouge, Resource One specializes in residential mortgage loans and is quickly becoming a key player in the industry's fast-paced commercial lending market. The company has accomplished this phenomenal growth by providing superior service and unprecedented customer satisfaction.

The firm is committed to making the loan process fast and easy, and represents more than 20 different investors, offering a wide array of financing options for any situation. The Resource One team specializes in conventional, FHA, VA, refinancing (both "cash out" and "rate/term"), new construction, and permanent financing loans. The firm also has an on-site underwriter.

The Resource One staff comprises a team of customer service specialists with diverse training and experience in areas such as real estate, banking, sales, financing, and marketing. Considering the company's collective experience, knowledge, and the financial diversity it offers, it comes as no surprise that Resource One has become a top volume mortgage broker in the south.

Bill Walker began his success story with just one office and three employees. Today, Resource One employs over 60 people with Louisiana offices in Baton Rouge, Denham Springs, Alexandria, Metairie, and Shreveport. Locations outside the state include offices in Gulf Shores, Alabama, Pensacola, Florida, and Jackson, Mississippi.

At Resource One, customer service is a priority. Personal attention is given to each client throughout the application process, from the first phone call to closing. However, customer service never really ends at Resource One, because the firm is not just content with "getting business." The company believes in keeping business and strives hard to achieve repeat and referral business.

"While Resource One is on the cutting edge of today's advanced technology, we still firmly believe that nothing takes the place of good, old fashioned customer service. Although our numbers reflect that of a huge brokerage firm, we still think of ourselves as the local guys who 'made good,'" said Sherry Denig, marketing director for the company.

Bill Walker adds, "In evaluating the sources in which our business originates, I'm pleased to see that we're not only seeing the same customers again and again, but they're also referring their friends, family members, and business associates. This in addition to our new business, leads me to believe that we must be doing something right."

It looks as if Walker chose the perfect name for his company. ✣

Gully, Phelps & McKey, Inc.

With roots that stretch back to the 1940s, Gully, Phelps & McKey, Inc. has established an impeccable reputation as the real estate firm to call in Baton Rouge for local market information and innovative services.

Built on a foundation of honesty, excellence, knowledge, and experience, Gully, Phelps & McKey is a locally-owned, full-service real estate firm specializing in residential and commercial sales, relocation, and new construction. The company heads a dynamic and successful team of more than 25 agents committed to continuing education and practicing the high standards set by the firm.

David McKey, Andrea Phelps McKey, Betty Phelps, R.B. McCall.

At Gully, Phelps & McKey success is easily measured in sales. Since 1989, the firm has sold more than 90 percent of its residential listings. The company attributes this success rate to a tremendous amount of community support and to agents who are knowledgeable about the real estate industry.

Success, of course, is also measured in experience, and the sales associates at Gully, Phelps & McKey are experienced in not just real estate. "Our agents have backgrounds in a wide array of professions and occupations. They come from all walks of life," said Betty Phelps, owner of the firm. "The benefit is they speak the same language... they can identify with our clients in a more personable way and provide better service." Their diverse experience enables them to meet the specific needs of each client.

Attention to customer service is a hallmark of Gully, Phelps & McKey. The firm believes in helping customers meet their individual real estate goals with as little stress as possible. Whether it's orienting newcomers to the Baton Rouge area or showing locals a shortcut to their new home, the firm's dedication to customer service is extraordinary.

Betty Phelps, President.

Originally named Gully & Phelps, the firm was founded in 1989 by two of the area's most respected names in real estate, Durward Gully and Betty Phelps. In addition to their civic work, both Realtors also brought an extensive list of accomplishments and knowledge about the local real estate market to the firm. Most notably, Gully, active in the local market since the 1940s, successfully developed many subdivisions and other residential communities throughout Baton Rouge, including Jefferson Terrace, Tara Place, Centurion Place, and Runnymede Townhomes.

In 1994, shortly after Gully's death, Phelps became the sole owner of Gully & Phelps. Today, operating as Gully, Phelps & McKey, the firm continues a tradition of excellence, working for the goal: "To Strive For The Best."

In that same spirit, partner David McKey is leading the firm's march into the next millennium. As an associate broker, manager, and state licensed residential contractor, McKey's expertise adds more diversification to Gully, Phelps & McKey, and gives it an edge in the burgeoning new construction markets of nearby Livingston and Ascension Parishes.

As the firm's youngest partner, McKey will also help provide the leadership needed to take Gully, Phelps & McKey into the future, while keeping it firmly rooted in the firm's core values of honesty and integrity.

"As we look to the future, it's important we not lose sight of our strengths," said McKey. "We are a very respected company;... we try to do things the way they should be done."

From the firm's very beginnings to today, that philosophy of "doing it right" has been important, and can best be exemplified by Phelps. From her first award as Rookie of the Year in 1971, to twice being recognized as Realtor of the Year by the Baton Rouge Board of Realtors and by the Louisiana Realtors Association, Phelps's industry honors continue to grow year after year. In turn, she has served the profession she loves in a number of highly visible posts, including president of the Louisiana Realtors Association and a regional vice president of the National Association of Realtors.

Phelps's strong commitment to her profession is only sidelined by her work for the community. She serves on the Better Business Bureau Board of Directors, the Campfire Board of Directors, and is an active member of the Rotary Club and other organizations. She also spearheaded the establishment of a scholarship at Louisiana State University. Given annually to a deserving student, the tuition award is presented in the memory of Durward Gully. ✦

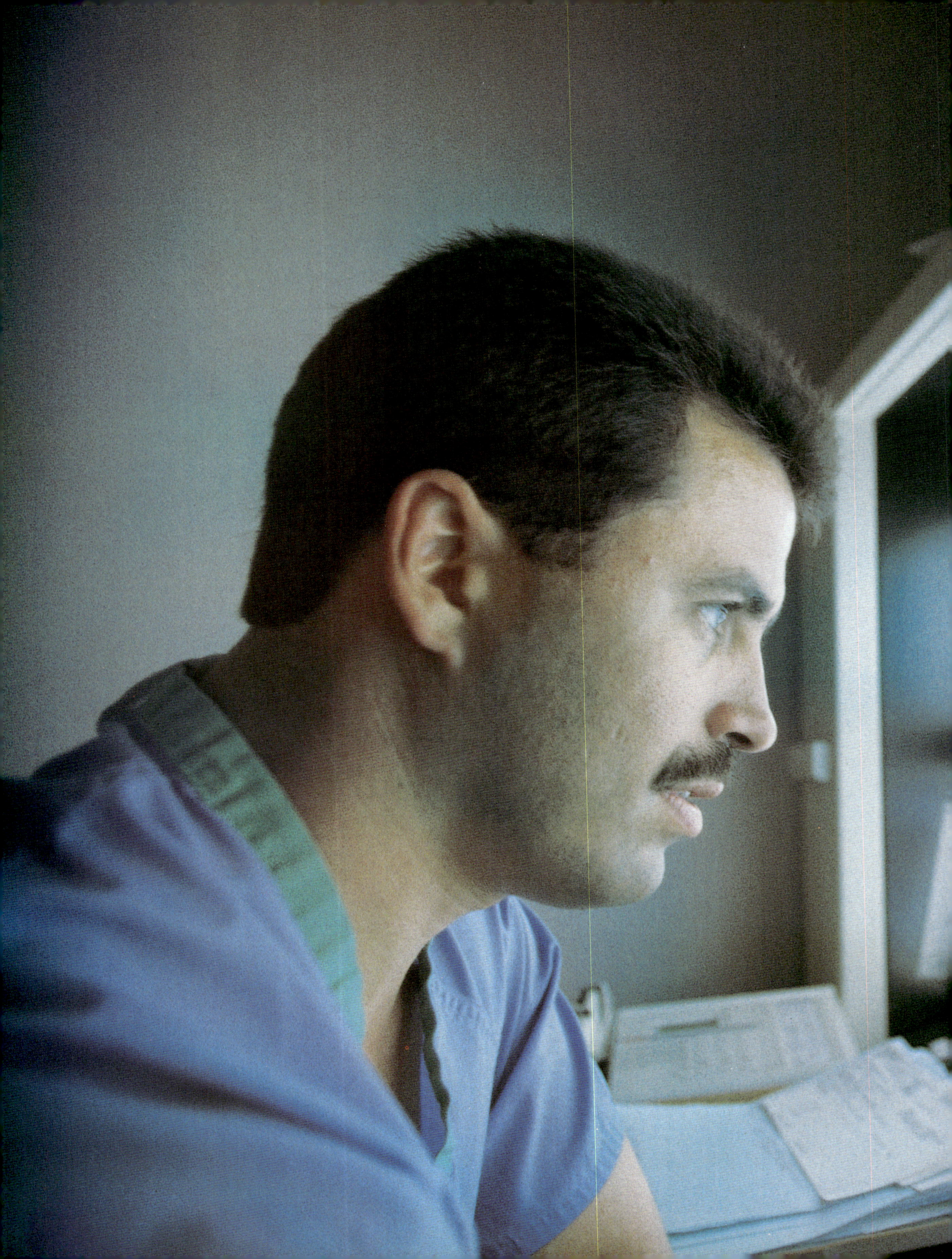

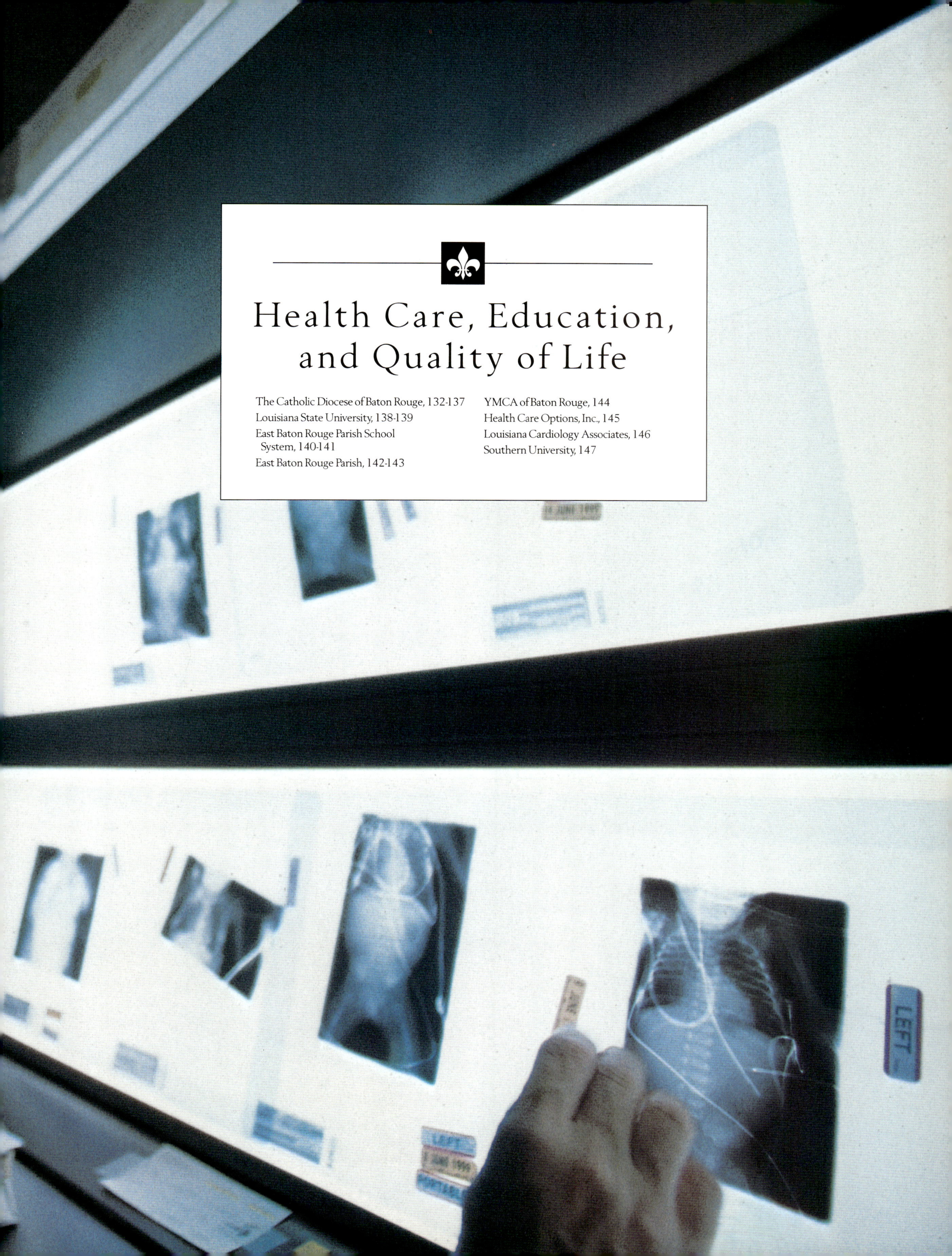

Health Care, Education, and Quality of Life

The Catholic Diocese of Baton Rouge

St. Joseph Cathedral, a Baton Rouge landmark, was one of the first cathedrals in the nation to complete renovation of an existing church in harmony with the provisions of the Constitution on Sacred Liturgy issued by Vatican Council II. Photo by Marie Constantin.

Like the city it serves, the Roman Catholic Diocese of Baton Rouge celebrates a history rich in tradition and culture. Created in 1961 through the initiative of the late Pope John XXIII, the Diocese of Baton Rouge is one of seven dioceses in the state of Louisiana. Though only established in the early 1960s, the Catholic heritage of this community actually dates back centuries ago, long before the city was even called Baton Rouge.

The earliest recorded history of the Catholic Church in this region begins with the writings of explorers and missionaries. In the wilderness of the so-called New World, Spanish and French missionaries followed the mandate of Christ to "Go therefore, teach ye all nations, baptizing them in the name of the Father, and of the Son, and of the Holy Spirit, teaching them to observe all things whatsoever I have commanded of you."

In time, the French explorer, Robert Cavelier, Sieur de La Salle claimed the Mississippi River and all the land that drained into it for France. On April 6, 1682, La Salle planted a cross at a point where the mighty river divides into three channels at its mouth which would later become part of the state of Louisiana.

Roger Baudier, in his book *The Catholic Church in Louisiana*, compares the planting of the cross by La Salle as "prophetic of the deep-rooted faith that was henceforth to develop in the state and to continue undying down the centuries."

Indeed, the time had come for planting the faith in Louisiana, and on March 3, 1699, journal records document the first Catholic Mass was celebrated on soil of what is now the state of Louisiana. Father Anastase Douay, a Recollect priest traveling with a group headed by the famous French brothers, Pierre Le Moyne, Sieur d'Iberville, and Jean Baptiste Le Moyne de Bienville, celebrated the Mass. The group was exploring the Mississippi River and the surrounding areas to help colonize the territory for France.

Interestingly, several days later, on March 17, 1699, while traveling upriver, Iberville and his crew spotted a large vertical pole, red with the blood of animals and fish heads attached to it. Tradition holds that Iberville named the spot *le Baton Rouge*, French for "red stick." Historians have since concluded that this pole probably served as a boundary marker between the Houma and Bayou Goula Indian tribes, natives to the region.

During this period, many other missionaries either worked or traveled through the area. One in particular, Father Paul du Ru, S.J. built the first church within the future diocesan boundaries. Located in what is now Iberville Parish, the chapel was built for the Bayou Goula Indians.

By 1718, France was eager to colonize the Baton Rouge area, and large grants of land, called concessions, were given out to anyone who agreed to settle the land. Bernard Diron d'Artaguette received one of these

On the first Sunday of Lent each year, hundreds of adults and children come to St. Joseph Cathedral to express to the Bishop their desire to join the Catholic Church. Photo by Laura Deavers.

concessions, and was the only owner at the time that did not abandon his property.

Four years later, Baton Rouge consisted of d'Artaguette's plantation and a few scattered huts built along the shores of a creek now known as Capitol Lake. It was in this habitation that an improvised altar was made on New Year's Day, 1722 for the celebration of the first Mass in Baton Rouge by Father Pierre Francois Xavier de Charlevoix, S.J., a noted historian, traveler, and scientist, who had stopped in Baton Rouge while making an official examination of the Canadian and Louisiana colonies for the French government.

And by coincidence, the place where Father Pierre celebrated Baton Rouge's first Mass is within the same area that now makes up St. Joseph Parish—the Cathedral Parish of the Diocese of Baton Rouge.

Certainly, few cathedral churches in America have had a more interesting history than St. Joseph's. During the 19th century, yellow fever epidemics, the Civil War, and Reconstruction besieged the parish. In fact, during the Battle of Baton Rouge in 1862, federal gunboats shelled the area around the church, and when the gunfire stopped, the parish's pastor, Father Frederic Larnaudie, S.J. was arrested, and held by Federal troops as a spy. He was later released.

Through the years, a total of three churches have served St. Joseph Parish. The first church was built in 1789 under the leadership of the area's first resident pastor, Father Carlos Burke, an Irish priest. The name of the parish at that time was Our Lady of Sorrows. The second church was erected in 1831 during the pastorate of Father Antoine Blanc, who later became the First Archbishop of New Orleans.

The third church to serve St. Joseph Parish is the present Cathedral. It was built in 1853, and was enlarged several times. In 1964, an extensive renovation plan was completed making the Diocese of Baton Rouge one of the first in the nation to complete renovation of an existing church in harmony with the provisions of the Constitution on the Sacred Liturgy issued by Vatican Council II.

Many nationalities have special liturgical services in keeping with their ethnic traditions. Representatives of the Hispanic countries present in the Diocese participate in a special Mass honoring the Blessed Mother. Photo by Laura Deavers.

St. Joseph's Church was named the Cathedral Church of the Diocese on November 8, 1961, the same day the Most Reverend Robert E. Tracy, D.D., L.L.D. was installed as First Bishop of Baton Rouge. At the time of Bishop Tracy's installation, the new Diocese of Baton Rouge encompassed some 50 parishes and served 150,000 Catholics.

Parish Life in the Diocese of Baton Rouge

Today, the Diocese of Baton Rouge serves almost 300,000 Catholics in 70 parishes and 20 mission chapels as well as two chaplaincies and Vietnamese and Hispanic apostolates. The Most Reverend Alfred C. Hughes, S.T.D., currently serves as the Fourth Bishop of Baton Rouge. He was installed on November 4, 1993.

The second bishop of Baton Rouge was the Most Rev. Joseph V. Sullivan, while Bishop Hughes' immediate predecessor was the Most Rev. Stanley Joseph Ott.

The Diocese of Baton Rouge comprises the civil parishes of Ascension, Assumption, East Baton Rouge, West Baton Rouge, Iberville, Pointe Coupee, East Feliciana, West Feliciana, St. Helena, Tangipahoa, Livingston, and St. James.

The church parishes, for the most part, are defined by geographical boundaries. There are several church parishes which are considered non-territorial parishes which have no geographic boundaries. Six parishes originally erected to serve the African American population are non-territorial. The rich racial and ethnic diversity of the Diocese is evident in the different liturgical styles of the Mass as it is celebrated by parishioners of French, Hispanic, African-American, Italian, German, Hungarian, Vietnamese, and many other ancestries. One non-territorial parish is dedicated to the pastoral care of the hearing-impaired and is located across the street from the State School for the Hearing-Impaired.

Each church parish has a pastor along with professionally trained lay people and religious, who serve in the variety of ministries that are called for in a parish. Twenty-five active permanent deacons serve in parishes as well as in specialized ministries, such as prisons and nursing homes.

Young people carry a large cross through the streets of the city as a sign of their faith. Photo by Laura Deavers.

Of the slightly more than 100 priests serving in the Diocese most are diocesan priests, but some 12 religious orders of priests also provide pastoral care. Some priests have also come from such countries as Ireland, India, the Philippines, Vietnam, Cuba, El Salvador, and Malta to serve in this diocese.

Church parishes nurture the sacramental life of the faithful primarily through the Mass. The reception of the other sacraments along with the pastoral and community activities of each parish builds a strong community, which is brought together because of their common faith.

Local Catholic Daughters of the Americas build a house for Habitat for Humanity. Photo by Laura Deavers.

The church parish is often the first place parishioners turn to in time of need. Whether in times of personal crisis or emergency assistance, Catholics know they can depend on their faith community.

Parish fairs and festivals, a part of the cultural life of many parishes, build up the faith community as parishioners work together for a common goal. *Allons manger* (Let's eat) is not only the name of one parish festival but the main attraction at all of these: crawfish, jambalaya, gumbo, boudin, muffolettas, spaghetti and meatballs, and red beans and rice. *Tous c'est bon.*

Parishes offer religious education for all of their members, from the very young to the very old, through parish schools of religion and adult continuing education programs. Each parish follows religious education guidelines set forth by the Diocesan Office of Religious Education concerning the material that must be taught and the proper training and certification of religious education teachers both in the parish and in Catholic schools. A special program, the Rite of Christian Initiation for Adults, provides information about the Catholic faith and formation to those who are interested in becoming members. Through the Diocesan Department of Christian Formation, lay persons are able to receive the education necessary to serve in various parish ministries.

Education in the Diocese of Baton Rouge

The vibrant life of many parishes also includes a parish elementary and high school since education has always played an important role in the Catholic Church.

Here in the Baton Rouge Diocese, Catholic schools have been preparing people for life in this world and in the next through a good education shaped by religious truth for more than 150 years. The first Catholic school in Baton Rouge opened in a residence at the corner of Florida and Fourth streets. Three nuns from the Daughters of Charity Religious Order founded the school, which was known as St. Mary's Academy. The sisters also began a Sunday morning catechism school for girls and a Sunday evening one for slaves. Over many years the administration of the school passed to the Madames of the Sacred Heart, the Christian Brothers, and the Sisters of St. Joseph of Medaille.

In addition to these religious orders many others have provided dedicated and unselfish service to the Diocese's education community over the years. These include Brothers of the Sacred Heart, Dominican Sisters of St. Mary, School Sisters of Notre Dame, Holy Family Sisters, Marianites of Holy Cross, Daughters of Jesus, Irish Dominican Sisters, Redemptorist Fathers, Salesian Sisters, Sisters of Mt. Carmel, Sisters of the Immaculate Conception, Sisters of the Holy Ghost, Sisters of the Most Holy Sacrament, and Springfield Dominican Sisters.

The Diocesan Catholic Schools Office is entrusted with the continuing development of exemplary elementary and secondary Catholic Schools in the community.

Today, there are 34 Catholic schools in the Diocese, comprising eight high schools, 26 elementary schools and two special education centers. There are more than 16,500 students enrolled throughout the Diocese in grades Pre-K - 12, comprising all races, religious backgrounds, and cultures. Students at every level receive a quality academic program. Students are exposed to religious instruction, daily prayer, sacramental preparation, service programs, and retreats, in a faith filled, and caring learning environment. In addition, students can elect to participate in a vast array of extracurricular activities.

Education has always played an important role in the Catholic Church. Catholic schools in the Diocese of Baton Rouge have offered a quality education for over 150 years. Photo by Marie Constantin.

In the Diocese, the most currently available statistics show 96 percent of graduating seniors in May, 1998 went on to college. The graduating seniors attending the eight Catholic high schools in the diocese, St. Joseph's Academy, St. Thomas Aquinas High School, St. John High School, Bishop Sullivan High School, Redemptorist High School, Catholic High School of Pointe Coupee, Catholic High School in Baton Rouge, and Ascension Catholic High School, received over $10 million in scholarships and saved their parents $325 thousand by receiving advanced credits in college courses.

In May 1999, the Diocese of Baton Rouge School Board won national recognition at the National Catholic Educational Association's annual convention. The National Association of Boards of Catholic Education recognized the board as one of seven in the country for their achievements in advancing and strengthening the future of Catholic education.

Two Catholic high schools in the Diocese, Catholic High School and St. Joseph's Academy, are National Schools of Excellence having received this honor from the U.S. Department of Education.

But it is not only in the elementary and high schools that the Church is concerned about the faith life of her children. On the campuses of Louisiana State University, Southern University, and Southeastern Louisiana University, the Church maintains Catholic Student Centers to provide a place where college students can nurture their faith and find camaraderie among other students. At Louisiana State University, Christ the King Parish has been providing spiritual life to students, faculty, and staff since 1929. Through the years, the ministry has grown, and today, 52 percent of the students on LSU's campus are Catholic, ranking it among the top five predominantly Catholic non-private higher education institutions in the United States.

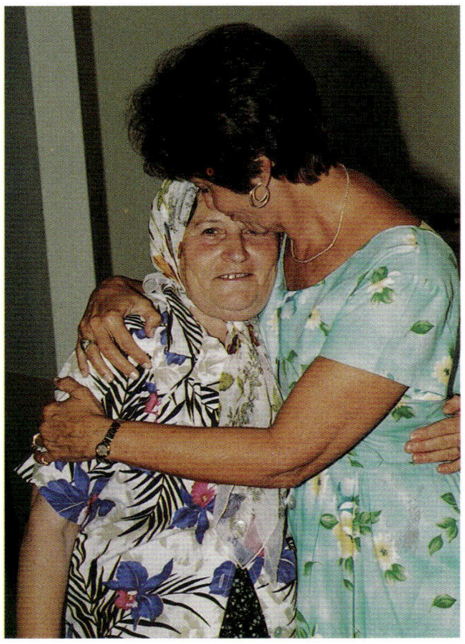

Refugees are made to feel welcome and safe as they are assisted in making a new home in this area. Photo by Laura Deavers.

Social Services in the Diocese of Baton Rouge

From its humble beginnings to today's community influence in the areas of religion, education, social outreach, health care, and spiritual development, the Catholic Church continues to serve as a source of strength and life for the people of Baton Rouge. Indeed, the Diocese of Baton Rouge ministers to the physical and emotional needs of thousands of men, women, and children daily, regardless of their faith.

The Church responds to the needs of individuals and families, especially the poor in the Diocese, by supplementing local, state, and federal agencies through a vast outreach program. Funded by the generosity of parishioners in the Diocese, the Diocese itself, as well as public funds, these programs play a vital role in society, many times serving as the only source of hope and understanding to those in need.

In a community as diverse as Baton Rouge, many programs are warranted to meet so many needs. Catholic Community Services (CCS), an affiliate of Catholic Charities USA, expresses the principal diocesan response through an array of comprehensive services. By providing these services in the entire Diocese, CCS acts daily on its mission to proclaim the Gospel teachings of Jesus Christ, and to work with church and community for justice, peace, and compassion in society.

Adoptive parents are able to find the joy of parenting through adoption services offered by the Diocese of Baton Rouge. Photo by AMI Photography.

Among the community services provided by CCS are many programs which address the social responsibility of the Church to her people, the needs of couples as they prepare for marriage and family life, and the services available to unwed parents faced with parenting their child or placing the child for adoption.

Responding to the social teachings of the Gospel, CCS provides for the resettlement of immigrants and refugees into this community. As citizens from other countries come to Baton Rouge to make a new home, CCS, through its Office of Migration and Refugee Services, offers language training, social services, counseling, job placement, family reunification, and citizenship preparation for immigrants and refugees. Starting with the influx of Vietnamese after the fall of Saigon, Migration Refugee Services has helped citizens from

Eastern Europe, Central America and Africa settle in this community.

CCS also offers assistance to persons with disabilities in building their own community networks through voluntary relationships with local citizens. As advocates for those with disabilities, CCS staff members work with the community agencies to provide for them so that they may more fully participate in the life of Baton Rouge.

The Catholic faith is spread and nurtured through the vibrant life of local church parishes. Photo by Marie Constantin.

When disaster strikes as it often does with hurricanes and flooding, CCS responds by providing disaster relief, emergency assistance, and transitional housing for families and individuals affected by the crisis.

Through its prison ministry, CCS is able to coordinate activities with prison chaplains at prisons as they reach out to prisoners, troubled youth, and ex-offenders, and to offer a halfway house for men who have been released from prison.

The stability of family life is of great importance to the Church. The Marriage and Family Life Department counsels individuals, married couples, and families experiencing difficulties.

The Office of Counseling, Maternity, and Adoption, which is part of CCS, offers help to women troubled by their pregnancies. It also provides counseling to the parents as well as temporary foster care for infants who will be adopted and licensed adoption placement for domestic, international, and special needs adoptions.

In addition to the work being offered by CCS, assistance is given through such entities as the Society of St. Vincent de Paul, the Missionaries of Charity (Mother Teresa's Order), the Franciscan Missionaries of Our Lady, the Sisters of St. Joseph, and through the Church parishes.

The Society of St. Vincent de Paul sponsors two thrift stores where people may purchase used items at reasonable prices. The St. Vincent de Paul Dining Room serves hot meals daily to individuals and families unable to meet this most basic need. The Bishop Stanley Joseph Ott Shelter, named after the third Bishop of Baton Rouge, provides shelter, counseling, and other provisions to homeless men. A free community pharmacy provides prescription and over the counter medications to people who are often faced with forgoing life-sustaining medications because they cannot afford them. Homeless men, women, and their children are able to use the day shelter as a refuge and a place for job counseling.

The Missionaries of Charity provide housing for homeless women and their children, while the Sisters of St. Joseph have a shelter for women who do not have children living with them, primarily women who have been released from prison. The Sisters also have a thrift store.

One of largest Catholic institutions of service to the people of Baton Rouge is Our Lady of the Lake Regional Medical Center (OLOL-RMC). Under the direction of the Franciscan Missionaries of Our Lady, OLOLRMC first opened in 1923, and has expanded many times during the past 75 years to meet the varied and changing medical needs of the Greater Baton Rouge community.

In many church parishes parishioners carry on the work of St. Vincent de Paul helping the homeless find shelter, the hungry find food, and providing clothing for those who have none. Social responsibility committees in the parishes also help those who are in need of food, clothing, shelter, jobs, transportation, financial assistance, and counseling.

The Diocesan Youth Office takes an active participation in several community sponsored programs to help young people grow up in a better community. Diocesan sponsored rallies, conferences, retreats, and youth-oriented activities allow young people an opportunity to learn more about their faith, grow in their faith, and share their faith with others.

The Diocese communicates to her people and the wider community important events in the Catholic Church locally, nationally and internationally through The Catholic Commentator, the newspaper of the Diocese of Baton Rouge, and through Real One, a weekly television program produced by the Diocesan Office of Communication.

Gospel choirs, as well as traditional choirs, bring music to Masses and other liturgical celebrations. Photo by Laura Deavers.

As the Diocese of Baton Rouge prepares for the future, new construction is providing office space for CCS, an overnight conference center, a new church for Christ the King, and larger student center at LSU.

French missionaries brought the Catholic faith to Louisiana some 300 years ago. A local priest portrays the scene of the landing of these missionaries in Bayou Goula. Photo by Julie Mickles.

Involvement in the Broader Community

The Catholic Diocese of Baton Rouge is fortunate to find itself located in an area in which church and state really do work well together for the good of the community.

As a member of the Louisiana Interchurch Conference, the Catholic Church participates in an effort to bring together Christian churches in ecumenical activities. As a participant in the Federation of Churches and Synagogues, the Catholic Church seeks to promote inter-faith cooperation.

The Greater Baton Rouge Food Bank provides food items to parishes that have food pantries to feed the hungry. Parish churches and schools regularly have food drives to replenish the food shelves at the Food Bank. They are assisted by such organizations as the Knights of Columbus.

The Diocese participates in the Character First Program established by the City-Parish and community leaders to instill moral values in children.

Several church parishes are part of a consortium to provide funding and workers to build low-income houses in support of Habitat for Humanity. The Catholic Daughters of the Americas, an organization of Catholic women, built a Habitat for Humanity house in a week.

WIN, or Working Interfaith Network, brings churches members together in a grassroots manner to work to improve their community. Through WIN, several Catholic churches have joined members of other faiths to find ways to improve the quality of education for our children, eliminate crime, reduce pollution, and address the needs that the members of neighborhoods perceive as the most pressing.

The generosity of the people of all faiths in Baton Rouge has rendered an enormous amount of time and money to the many worthwhile efforts in the area, providing for a community that cares about its people.

Like the missionaries who planted the cross in Louisiana centuries ago, the missionaries of today carry the message of faith to the community through their service to the people, continuing to keep Baton Rouge strong on its journey into the new millennium.

These construction projects are possible because of The Campaign for Tomorrow, a capital campaign conducted by the Diocese in the late 1990s and designed to help the Diocese of Baton Rouge provide for its continued growth and meet the needs of future generations. The Campaign for Tomorrow also includes the establishment of an Educational Trust Fund for students in Catholic schools.

Bishop Alfred C. Hughes, fourth bishop of Baton Rouge, and Sister Mary Michaeline Green O.P., superintendent of Catholic Schools, gather with distinguished graduates of Catholic Schools from throughout the Diocese. Each year, the Diocese recognizes one graduate from each school for the honor of Distinguished Graduate.

Louisiana State University

Original campus architecture at LSU was based on the Renaissance domestic style of northern Italy and features tan stucco walls with red tile roofs. The Campanile, often called "the clock tower" is the memorial offered by LSU students and the people of Louisiana to those who lost their lives in World War I.

As the flagship university of the State of Louisiana and a nationally recognized research institution, LSU plays a vital role in the education and training of the people who create and nurture Baton Rouge's growing economy and civic awareness.

Under the leadership of Chancellor Mark Emmert and as one of eight institutions in the LSU System, the University is committed to providing and maintaining a standard of excellence in higher education.

Located on more than 2,000 acres bordered by the Mississippi River, the University is designated as a Research University I—the top category of the Carnegie Foundation's ranking of research institutions. The Research I designation, which is shared by only 59 public and 29 private universities in the country, places LSU in the top two percent of the nation's colleges and universities.

LSU is also one of only 25 universities in the country designated as both a land-grant and sea-grant institution. As such, the university is actively involved in research on both land and sea.

Interestingly, LSU can trace its ocean research efforts back to the 1950s with the creation of the University's Coastal Studies Institute, a multidisciplinary research unit still active today. As home to several of the world's foremost scientists in marine and coastal research, LSU is considered a vital component in the world's efforts to better understand the seas.

Other multidisciplinary research units at LSU include the Center for Coastal, Energy, & Environmental Resources (CCEER), the Center for Advanced Microstructures and Devices (CAMD), the National Ports and Waterways Institute, and the Office of Sea Grant Development.

In all, more than 35 institutes, centers for advanced study, and other specialized units are headquartered at LSU. Various state and federal governmental units also have offices and laboratories on campus.

Research at LSU is conducted by faculty and staff in academic departments and through organized research and public service units. Led by Vice Chancellor for Research & Graduate Studies Lynn Jelinski, more than 2,000 sponsored research projects are underway on campus at any given time.

In addition, faculty, staff, and graduate students pursue numerous research projects that are not sponsored by outside agencies. University researchers also conduct research projects and instructional programs through the LSU Agricultural Center; the Louisiana Agricultural Experiment Station, which includes 16 outlying research stations; and the Pennington Biomedical Research Center.

It is this creation of new knowledge that helps propel the economy of Baton Rouge and the state. Each year, LSU receives an average of $85 million in grants and contracts from federal, state, and private sources. In addition, the University injects more than $500 million into the Baton Rouge economy annually with direct expenditures of more than $344 million by all units in Baton Rouge, creating sales of nearly $672 million.

Of course, in order to continue and expand this economic enhancement, facilities must be in place to support various levels of ongoing research at LSU. The University's answer: the LSU Libraries.

Ranked 45th in size among the top research libraries in the nation, the LSU Libraries contain holdings of 2.9 million volumes, 3.5 million microforms, and more than 12 million manuscripts, with annual expenditures of more than $9 million.

The LSU Libraries comprise the main collection in the Troy H. Middleton Library, as well as the Chemistry Library and the Design Resource Center. In addition, Special Collections, which are housed in the Hill Memorial Library, contain an internationally recognized center for research in various fields including the history and culture of Louisiana and the lower Mississippi River region.

Another LSU Library that has received considerable attention is the LSU Law Library.

The beauty and charm of LSU captures the attention of many first-time visitors to the campus.

A Coastal Studies Institute researcher is lowered in a submersible to search for gas hydrates in the Gulf of Mexico. LSU is leading the way in researching the possibility of converting these gas hydrates, or domes of frozen methane gas, into tomorrow's energy resource.

Described as a "national treasure," the LSU Law Library has been recognized by the American Bar Association Accreditation Committee for its foreign and comparative law collections.

LSU in Baton Rouge is one of eight institutions in the LSU System established by the Louisiana Legislature in 1965. In 1998, former LSU Chancellor William Jenkins was named president of the LSU System. Two other units of the LSU System—the LSU Agricultural Center and the Paul M. Hebert Law Center—are also housed on the Baton Rouge campus.

The University is accredited by the Commission on Colleges of the Southern Association of Colleges and Schools to award bachelor's, master's, doctoral, and professional degrees.

LSU offers bachelors degrees in 73 major fields through the Colleges of Agriculture, Arts & Sciences, Basic Sciences, E.J. Ourso Business Administration, Design, Education, Engineering, General College, Music & Dramatic Arts, and the Manship School of Mass Communication. Master's degrees in 75 major fields and doctoral degrees in 55 major fields are offered through the Graduate School; the School of Veterinary Medicine offers the D.V.M. degree.

LSU alumni have distinguished themselves in politics, agriculture, business, education, engineering, science, the arts, sports, and entertainment. LSU ranks in the top 10 percent in the nation in the number of graduates.

Who enrolls at LSU? More than 29,000 students from all 50 states and more than 120 foreign countries attend LSU. Campus life today includes a broad spectrum of cultural and recreational activities as well as a vibrant student-run media, Greek system, and intercollegiate sports programs for men and women.

As a charter member of the Southeastern Conference (SEC), the Fighting Tigers meet teams from other major universities in NCAA Division 1A competition for football, baseball, men's and women's basketball, indoor and outdoor track and field, cross country, golf, tennis, swimming, and women's gymnastics, volleyball, soccer, and softball.

First-time visitors to LSU will immediately be struck by the campus' incredible beauty. Richly designed buildings based on the Renaissance domestic style of northern Italy create a picturesque skyline as do rows and rows of massive oak trees.

These trees, so synonymous with LSU, also define the rich history of the University, a history that began in 1853 when LSU was founded by the General Assembly of Louisiana as the Louisiana State Seminary of Learning and Military Academy near Pineville, Louisiana.

The institution opened on January 2, 1860, with five professors and 19 cadets. However, when the Civil War began, the school was closed temporarily.

Interestingly, the school's president at this time, William Tecumseh "War is Hell" Sherman, left to take a command in the Union Army while his students joined Confederate forces. During the war's Red River Campaign, when Union troops devastated the area, Sherman was credited with giving the order that saved the Seminary from massive destruction.

Soon after the war, the Seminary opened again in 1865; however, a fire forced it to close four years later. It was then moved to Baton Rouge, and renamed Louisiana State University in 1870. In 1877, LSU again changed its name to the Louisiana State University and Agricultural and Mechanical College after merging with the Louisiana State Agricultural and Mechanical College which had been established only three years earlier in New Orleans.

In the decades that followed, the school would face two more moves before calling its present campus home. Formal dedication of the present campus took place on April 30, 1926.

From its rich history and tradition, LSU has evolved into today's center of research and educational excellence. The University continues to serve as the nucleus for Baton Rouge, and as this Capital City embraces the 21st Century, LSU will also continue to fulfill its mission of providing for the generation, preservation, dissemination, and application of knowledge and cultivation of the arts for the benefit of the people of the state, the nation, and the global community. ⚜

Students watch a demonstration of a clay facial reconstruction. The University's Forensic Anthropology Computer Enhancement Services (FACES) Lab routinely assists law enforcement agencies from around the state and the country in rebuilding a face of clay from skeletal remains. This procedure helps officials identify missing persons. The FACES Lab is a satellite site of the National Center for Missing and Exploited Children. LSU is the only university linked to this site.

East Baton Rouge Parish School System

Quality. Equity. Excellence. These are the standards by which the East Baton Rouge Parish School System operates. Serving the entire Greater Baton Rouge area, including the cities of Baker and Zachary, the school system provides challenging educational opportunities for a vast array of students and plays a key role in the training of the community's next generation of business and civic leaders.

With an enrollment of approximately 56,000 students in Pre-kindergarten through Grade 12, and an additional 5,000 students in adult education, the East Baton Rouge Parish School System is the second-largest school district in the state, and among the top 60 nationally in student enrollment. Students from all walks of life participate in a strong academic curriculum enriched with art, music, computer technology, the foreign languages, and athletics.

Reaching a diverse population of students, the school system encourages the abilities of each child through academic settings in regular, gifted, talented, magnet, special education, and vocational education classes.

Recent academic gains and accomplishments show students in the East Baton Rouge Parish School System are meeting high expectations. ACT (American College Test) scores exceed the state average and are higher than 57 out of 66 school systems in the state. Graduation Exit Exam scores also surpass the state average, and according to enrollment figures, more students are now enrolling in college preparatory courses.

On the elementary level, reading scores for 2nd and 3rd grade students have been very impressive. Not only do these scores surpass identical test scores from surrounding parishes, but a comprehensive program developed and implemented recently in Pre-K through second grade has dramatically increased the number of students reading above grade level. The program incorporates work in both reading/language arts and mathematics and strives to teach every student to read and numerate by the end of the second grade. Since it began, the program has increased the number of students reading above grade level at the end of first grade by 32 percent and at the end of second grade by 76 percent.

Not surprisingly, the most recent test scores available from the IOWA exam, a norm referenced test that measures general achievement and compares East Baton Rouge students to a national sample of students, are also up. Student testing completed in the Spring of 1999 showed improvements in almost every subject and grade level. One of the most impressive achievements, scoring well above the state's goal, was language arts results from the school system's third grade students.

As technology continues to change our society, the school system is determined to equip students with the knowledge necessary to meet the challenges of tomorrow. In 1997, a five-year technology plan was implemented to improve the schools technology ratio from 16 students to five students per one computer. In addition, all schools have Internet access, and students are encouraged to regularly incorporate the use of technology in other fields of study.

Recognizing that the teaching profession makes all other professions possible, the East Baton Rouge Parish School System emphasizes the importance of teacher training and excellence in its 100 schools. Teachers are provided support and assistance in all areas of professional development including opportunities for advanced education and access to the school system's Christa McAuliffe Sherwood Center Computer Lab. Here, at this

state-of-the-art computer-training lab, teachers are given hands-on classes in the use of productivity software and how to integrate this technology into learning activities with their students. Of the more than 7,000 employees in the school system, more than half are certified principals, teachers, and guidance counselors.

Since the mid-90s, school system administrators have implemented a series of unprecedented changes in East Baton Rouge Parish public schools. These changes which include eliminating forced busing and restoring community attendance zones have led to increased community support. In 1997, a mandatory school uniform policy was enacted for elementary school students joined by a similar policy for middle school students two years later. School officials have found that uniforms allow students to focus more on academics, promote higher self-esteem, and result in a more orderly school campus.

Another change the community has embraced is the school system's Zero Tolerance for Fighting Policy. Instituted during the 1996-97 school year, the anti-violence policy brought immediate results, producing a 76 percent reduction in fighting. Before Zero Tolerance, 24 students per day were involved in fights at parish public schools. Today, averages of five students per day (out of a student body of approximately 56,000) are involved in fighting, and that number continues to fall.

Ever true to its past examples, the school system continues to implement new programs for educational improvement, and by all accounts the community is responding positively. For example, School Improvement Teams (groups of active parents, educators, business and religious leaders, and concerned citizens on all school campuses who have joined together to generate community involvement and improve education) are working on their goals of improved academics, discipline, and greater parental involvement. Called one of the most exciting efforts underway in parish public schools, School Improvement Teams serve as a voice of the community, placing the needs of the each student first.

In addition to the School Improvement Teams, the school system is also actively engaged in Reaching for Results, an accountability program designed to bring the state into conformity with the national emphasis on school accountability and make learning content more relevant. Through Reaching for Results, students are assisted in achieving higher level thinking skills and then learn how to apply that knowledge to real world situations.

But perhaps one of the school system's most notable accomplishments so far in advancing education in Baton Rouge is the opportunity it has been given to continue school improvements. In November 1998, voters approved three separate sales taxes to support East Baton Rouge Parish Schools. The sales tax plan was the first of its kind to pass in 30 years. All total, these taxes equal a one-cent sales tax increase that will be levied for five years. Money collected will be used to support school repairs and renovations, construct new classrooms, add technology, and build four new schools in the system including Woodlawn High School, Northeast Elementary School, Capitol Middle School, and Northeast Middle/High School. In addition, the sales tax is also earmarked to improve employee pay and to support discipline programs at elementary, middle, and high schools, as well establish a second alternative school for over-age middle school students and provide staff for a truancy center.

Certainly, by emphasizing achievement and success, the parish school system is preparing for the future and for the next generation of leaders in Baton Rouge. With community support firmly by its side, the school system is one step ahead in providing a quality education so all students in the East Baton Rouge Parish Schools can lead full, productive, and rewarding lives. ✤

East Baton Rouge Parish

The city parish government of East Baton Rouge Parish is playing an integral part in the strength of Baton Rouge's bustling economy—paving the way for continued growth and prosperity well into the 21st century through what Mayor President Tom Ed McHugh calls "the wheels that make it a smooth ride."

"I see government as serving a very strong role in the strength of the city's economy," said Mayor McHugh. "Through the actions of government, a climate is produced where business people can prosper. It's a team effort."

And the city parish government is definitely a team player. With offices downtown in the city's center, Mayor McHugh and his administration, along with the elected members of the Metropolitan City Council, focus daily on initiatives that address local issues and encourage entrepreneurial enterprises. City officials also contribute to the efforts of a broad coalition of private citizens, community groups, and businesses that seek to make Baton Rouge one of the country's most desirable places in which to work and raise a family.

One of the most important components in any American city is public safety, and since taking office in 1989, Mayor McHugh has placed a great deal of emphasis on improving the city's Fire, Police, and Emergency Medical Services (EMS). From providing more departmental funding to offering incentives, such as additional pay for officers earning a college degree, the efforts have now been fully realized, marking a major milestone in Baton Rouge's 300-year history.

Based on accreditation processes completed individually by each department, East Baton Rouge Parish has been awarded the top national ratings in fire protection, police protection, and EMS. The national professional appraisals were based on achieving high marks in such areas as response time, equipment, and manpower.

Certainly, earning a top classification for any one of the city's public safety departments is an honor in itself, but to be recognized for superior abilities in all three sectors places Louisiana's Capitol City in a select group of the nation's best cities. For Baton Rouge businesses and residents, this number one rating is very important and the advantages are plentiful, including lower insurance premiums.

"The (insurance) system is indicative of where you live. Obviously, if you live in an area where the fire department is not rated, then you pay more. As for us, you just can't get any better than a number one rating," said Mayor McHugh.

The parish's public safety component also extends into the city's emergency management department. Here, state-of-the-art technology is used to assist the city's police department, fire department, and EMS in handling major city emergencies, such as hurricane preparations. Upgraded communication systems give firefighters, police officers, and EMS technicians the ability to simultaneously communicate with regards to any emergency situation, ensuring the most appropriate help arrives in the fastest time possible.

Technology has also improved response time thanks to the addition of a new vehicle location system, which provides information on the whereabouts of every emergency vehicle at any given time. But perhaps one of the most important technological improvements in public safety has been the addition of laptops on every fire truck. Using a computer, firefighters now have immediate access to the building layout of every major business, commercial area, school, university, or governmental entity. This information also benefits fire officials in developing preplanning techniques or training skills.

"Not many cities are as far advanced as we are when it comes to using technology in public safety. We're on the front edge in all aspects of technology," said Mayor McHugh.

The parish is also on the leading edge when it comes to finishing a massive rehabilitation project of its streets and roads. A combination of wear and hazardous weather conditions prompted the refurbishing or new construction of over 1,200 miles of roads and streets in the parish. Shortly after McHugh was elected Mayor, citizens approved and subsequently renewed a one half-cent sales tax to take care of the problem. Rehabilitation works started in 1990, and as of June 1999, more than two-thirds of all parish roadways, more than 1,192 miles, are rehabilitated.

"This (rehabilitation of the streets and roads) is a very positive thing. By putting our roads and streets in excellent condition, we are providing a good foundation for the future," said Mayor McHugh.

The future is also expected to be even stronger for the city's center. Several years ago, concerned residents and business leaders watched as Baton Rouge began to follow the pattern of other urban cities shifting its focus away from the city's downtown area. Recognizing the historical importance of Baton Rouge's downtown area and its prized location near the Mississippi River, organizations such as the Downtown Development District, the Baton Rouge Area Foundation, PLAN Baton Rouge, the Greater Baton Rouge Chamber of Commerce, and the state of Louisiana began to work together to revitalize the downtown area.

Since that time, from 1987 to 1998, downtown Baton Rouge has seen more than $340 million in public and private investments. In 1999 alone, downtown Baton Rouge will have approximately $151 million in public and private capital investments. Some of the many areas of progress include refurbishing the Old State Capital, adding a planetarium and Omni-Max theatre at the Louisiana Arts and Science Center, and completing a $40 million expansion of the Riverside Centroplex and Exhibition Hall, which will provide Baton Rouge with the infrastructure needed to attract larger conventions.

"It is important to revitalize downtown Baton Rouge because it is the heart and soul of our community, and as such, it is a reflection of our city," said Davis Rhorer, executive director, Downtown Development District. "Right now, we are on the verge of making great strides downtown. I feel very confident the future will be a bright and bold one for our community."

As East Baton Rouge Parish faces the next century, it will continue to see new development in its city center, and by capitalizing on what it does best and focusing on its assets, such as public safety and the Mississippi River, the parish's potential is already attracting attention. In 1999, *Forbes Magazine* ranked Baton Rouge as the 40th best place in America to do business. No doubt the magazine editors noticed what Mayor McHugh and other locals have known all along, "great things are happening in this city." ✤

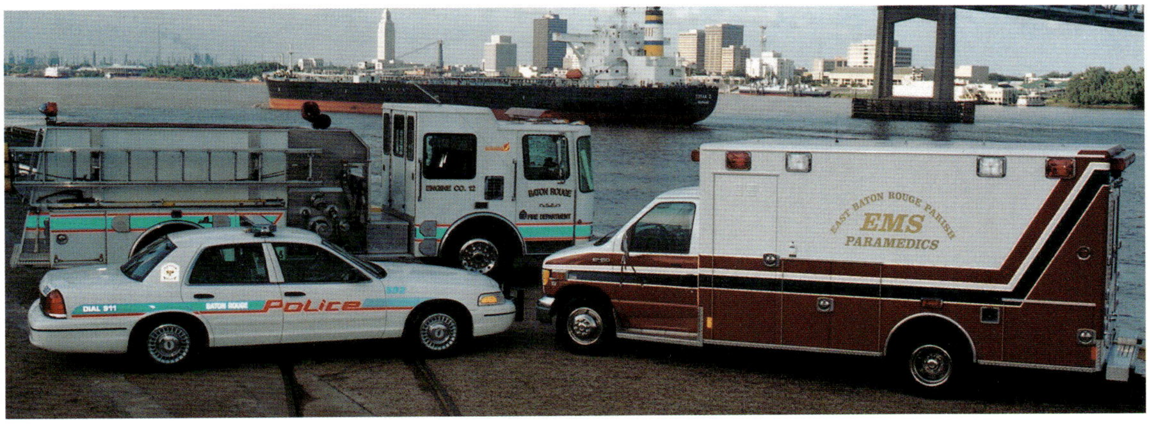

YMCA of Baton Rouge

As an international organization, the Young Men's Christian Association, or YMCA as it has come to be called, yields a distinct and highly respectable image. Founded more than 150 years ago in London, England, the YMCA has long been a place known for recreation and family fun.

But today's "Y" has become more than just a place to take swim lessons or play sports. Yes, basketball was invented by a Massachusetts YMCA gym instructor in 1861, and sports continue to be a focus of the organization. But through the years, and in an effort to reach every level of society, the "Y" has introduced programs, activities, and classes that not only enrich but also nurture every member of the community. Indeed, the YMCA has become woven into the fabric of our American culture.

And nowhere is that more evident than here in Baton Rouge.

For more than eight decades, since 1917, the Baton Rouge YMCA has been serving the local community, offering programs and services that include what many would label the more traditional YMCA activities, such as sports teams and state-of-the-art fitness facilities, to the more unique and community-oriented, such as after school care, meals on wheels, and a teen center.

Everyday the Baton Rouge YMCA, according to Jacobs, serves more than 1,200 people. These people either attend programs or receive services from one of the four YMCA branches in the community. The four extensions are the Baranco-Clark Branch located on Thomas Delpit Drive; the A.C. Lewis Branch located on S. Foster Drive; the Paula G. Manship Branch located near Perkins Road and Seigen Lane; and the C.B. Pennington, Jr. Branch located on Old Hammond Highway.

"All of our branches are strategically located throughout the community to better meet the needs of each individual. While we do offer similar programs at every extension, such as senior programs and day camp, each branch is also unique in that specific programs are offered only at certain locations depending on the needs of the area," explains Jacobs.

What are some of these more unique programs and activities? The list, which is quite extensive, includes massage therapy, gymnastics, scuba, yoga, fitness testing, children's dance, and Black Achievers, a mentoring program for junior and high school students.

Another program that has generated much excitement in Baton Rouge is a ropes challenge course. Offered only at the Paula G. Manship Branch, the course contains 22 high and low rope elements including a climbing wall.

The ropes challenge course is also a very popular program with local teenagers, a group the Baton Rouge YMCA is working hard to attract. Recognizing that young people today are often bombarded with conflicting and many times unhealthy messages from today's culture, the Baton Rouge YMCA has chosen to expand its teen programming so young people can have choices.

"We have a 'Highland Club' at the Manship Branch. It's our first teen club. You can also call it a safe-haven," says Pat Hanchey, marketing director of the Baton Rouge YMCA.

Hanchey added that the "Highland Club" is a place where teenagers can come to do things together. Of course, they can swim and play sports, but they also have their own governing board. Timely activities for teenagers even include study-help preparations for the ACT (a college entrance exam), as well as tailgating at LSU football games.

The Baton Rouge YMCA also participates in another program for youth. Called "Youth in Government," this nationwide YMCA program began in Louisiana in 1962. Since that time, thousands of young people in the state have been able to learn more about the legislature through active participation.

In 1987, Model United Nations Conference was also added.

Participation in all programs offered by the Baton Rouge YMCA is open to the entire community. In keeping with the organization's mission of uniting in a common effort to enhance the quality of life, spiritually, mentally, physically, and socially for all people in the community through the ecumenical application of Christian principles, the Baton Rouge YMCA offers scholarships to assist those families in need.

"Our 'Kids Under Construction' program is one example. These are scholarships funded through individual or business donations so kids who don't have the (financial) ability can still attend summer camp," explains Jacobs.

"Here at the 'Y', we don't want to turn people away based simply on their inability to pay," Jacobs adds.

The Baton Rouge YMCA is also one of 57 agencies in the community that is a United Way agency. Contributions through the United Way play an integral part in enabling the "Y" to reach every level of need in the community. Various social services are offered on a daily basis and touch thousands of people in the area.

Of course, much of what the "Y" is able to accomplish is reached primarily by the help of volunteers. Hundreds of people from all walks of life actively fulfill the mission of the YMCA everyday. From coaching t-ball and other sports to helping deliver much-needed social services in the community, these volunteers are a valuable asset to the orgaization.

"We have outstanding volunteers. Without their continued support, we would not be able to do the kinds of things that we do," Jacobs says.

"At the YMCA, we build strong kids, strong families, and strong communities." ⚜

Health Care Options, Inc.

Established from a genuine belief that every human being has worth and every individual should receive proper medical care, regardless of income level, race, age, religion, or sex, Health Care Options (HCO) provides a full range of quality home health care services in Baton Rouge and the surrounding areas. Locally owned by Annette Evans Austin, RN, BSN, MBA and Howard Douglas Austin, the firm's obvious humanitarian philosophy is derived specifically from the background of Annette Austin.

As a young girl growing up in Mississippi, Annette sympathized with the pain of others, especially the elderly, living without adequate access to hospitals and clinics. Years later, while working as a Registered Nurse, and later, as the Director of Nursing for a home health care program, she knew she could make a difference in the lives of the medically needy. From that personal ministry of care and service, Annette opened an office in her home with her husband, Douglas and thus, Health Care Options was founded in 1986.

Today, HCO is a national leader in the home health industry, offering a full spectrum of quality health care services. The company continues to expand its approach to health care delivery and has proven its ability to provide an array of services, some quite unique in the field of home health care. HCO employs more than 250 dedicated health care professionals and administrative staff members. In 1999, the *Greater Baton Rouge Business Report* ranked Health Care Options the largest minority owned business in the city, based upon the number of employees.

In 1997, HCO began operating under the umbrella of Austin Technical Companies, an integrated family of professional healthcare companies. Other Austin Technical Companies include: The Helping Center, a community mental health center providing a partial-hospitalization program for psychiatric patients; Global Health Management Systems, Inc., one of the south's leading healthcare consulting firms offering a comprehensive training and conference center; HCO Nursing Services Inc.; and the Jackson, Mississippi-based Choices for Children Health Care Clinic, which provides vital routine screenings such as hearing, vision, dental, and physical assessments of children.

Health Care Options Corporate Office. Health Care Options is one of the most noted and respected home health organizations in Southern Louisiana.

Since its founding, HCO has remained committed to its mission of providing caring, compassionate, and competent services to help individuals attain and maintain their highest possible functional capacity given the constraints of their illness or handicap. HCO provides the utmost in quality medical care and has received full accreditation from the Joint Commission on Accreditation of Healthcare Organizations (JCAHO), which emphasizes the highest standards in healthcare.

Through the company's Skilled Nursing Department, medical professionals receive continuous training and education in the very latest technological advances for home health care. In 1994, after recognizing a need for further expertise in certain areas of home health, HCO developed the Nurse Specialty Program, which provides additional training and skills for nurses in such areas as Geriatrics, Diabetes, Urology, Pediatrics, Rehabilitation, Orthopedics, Cardiology, Psychiatric Nursing, and Oncology.

Always striving to further meet the needs of the community, HCO also developed specialized training and specialty programs for its home care aides. From Physical Therapy to care of the diabetic patient and Alzheimer's Disease, home care aides are further educated to assist other clinical staff members by remaining watchful of a patient's condition.

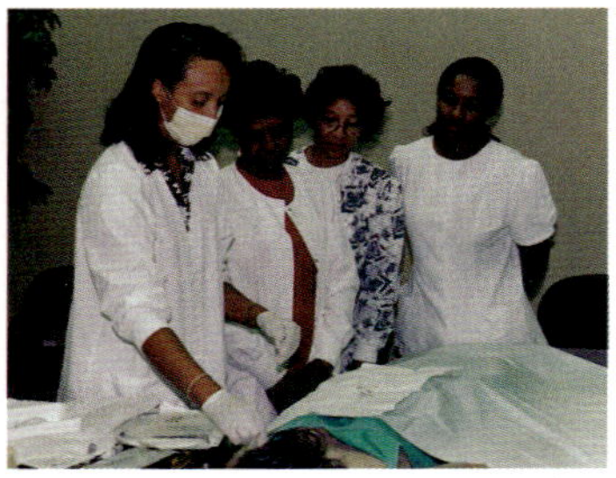

Health Care Options' expert staff, coupled with caring, compassion, and competence makes a first-class organization.

At HCO, a holistic approach to total patient care is supported. As such, the company provides home health care services in occupational, physical and speech therapy, medical social services, and psychiatric home care services.

HCO and Austin Technical Companies have geared up to meet the multi-faceted challenges and opportunities in the future of health care. The firm has already embarked on an electronic transfer of information to speed administrative paperwork and ultimately assist in providing more effective and efficient patient care. While the delivery of health care continues to transform amid technological advances, health care alliances, and governmental regulations, HCO remains diligent. Assisted by its branch offices in Plaquemine, Gonzales, Lafayette, and Jackson, Louisiana, the company continues to focus on new and better ways of providing quality health care, especially to those who are the most needy. Ever committed to the company's founding principles of care, compassion, and competence, HCO is determined to make a difference and firmly believes in its motto of "Bringing Tomorrow's Healthcare Home Today." ✤

Louisiana Cardiology Associates

In 1965, Dr. David Wall came to Baton Rouge to practice cardiology. During the late 1960's and continuing from then on, technological advances appeared rapidly in cardiology requiring the cardiologist in practice to

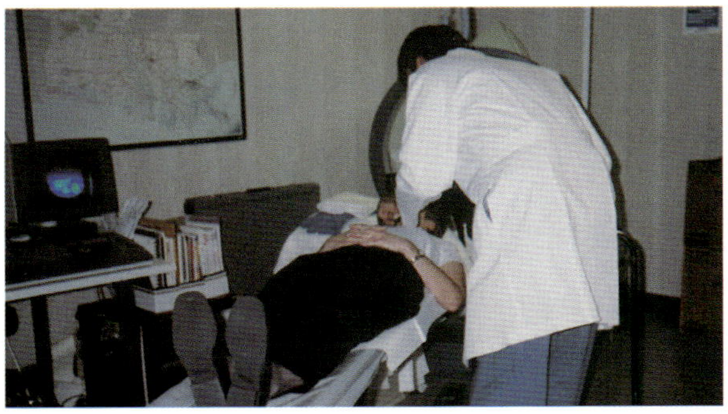

purchase equipment to keep current with these advances. Treadmill machines, holter monitors, and echocardiogram machines were extremely useful pieces of equipment but expensive and they required multiple cardiologists to be able to afford their purchase. In addition to the equipment needed in the office, the local development of high-quality cardiac catheterization laboratories and open-heart surgery programs in the local hospitals, greatly expanded the role of the cardiologist. Dr. Harris Lappin came to Baton Rouge in 1975 and the two cardiologists started working together, as associates, and then joined together to form Louisiana Cardiology Associates in June of 1976. In July of 1976, Drs. Jeffrey Moonan and Tom Quaid came to Baton Rouge and joined the group, and Dr. Terry Rehn was added in 1977, making a five man cardiology group. Eventually, by 1997, the Louisiana Cardiology Associates had grown to include eleven doctors, all committed to the same mission of promoting the prevention of cardiovascular disease and providing comprehensive cardiac care in a timely and cost-efficient manner with warmth and compassion. The group operates two primary offices in Baton Rouge located on Dijon Drive and Florida Boulevard respectively, a third office in Gonzales and satellite offices in St. Francisville and Brusly. In addition, Louisiana Cardiology provides consultative services and teaching services at Earl K. Long Hospital. In 1997, the Joint Commission on Accreditation for Healthcare Organization, which accredits hospitals, moved into accrediting physicians' offices on a voluntary basis, and Louisiana Cardiology Associates (LCA) was the first group of physicians across the southeastern states whose office practice was accredited by this organization.

LCA offers patient care in all aspects of adult cardiovascular disease. The group is committed to staying abreast of current research and providing a staff of physicians skilled in such advanced areas of cardiovascular medicine as nuclear medicine, new intervention procedures, echocardiography technology, and electrophysiology. All of the cardiologists were trained in invasive techniques including angioplasty and balloon angioplasty and the new options of balloon angioplasty such as laser therapy and stent placement. In fact, two doctors in practice, Drs. N. Joseph Deumite and Steven Gremillion, were trained in electrophysiological techniques and helped develop the services in the hospital. Prior to this development, patients requiring electrophysiological studies had to travel elsewhere.

Physicians on staff at Louisiana Cardiology Associates also share their knowledge and expertise with the community in many ways. As mentioned, all doctors in the group are on the LSU teaching staff at Earl K. Long Hospital. The physicians of LCA have been elected to leadership roles in the medical community. Dr. Wall was in charge of professional education for the Louisiana Heart Association (now American Heart Association Louisiana) for

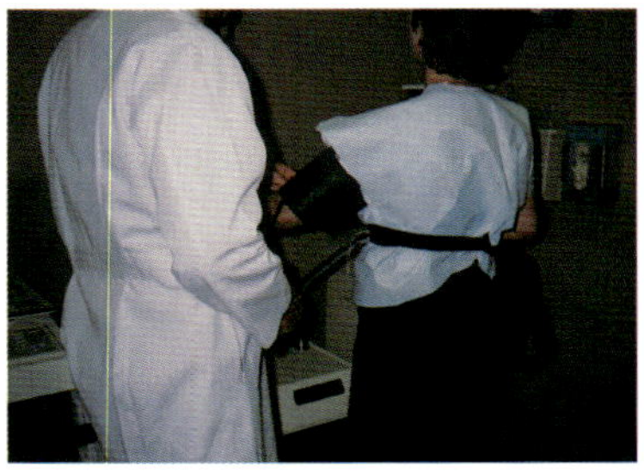

seven years and then became president of the organization for one year. Dr. Harris Lappin served two terms as chief of staff at the Baton Rouge General Hospital and Dr. John McClelland served as chief of staff at Our Lady of the Lake Regional Medical Center.

With its entire staff of physicians, nurses, technicians, and office personnel, Louisiana Cardiology Associates is committed to providing a continuum of care for each patient, emphasizing the patient/doctor relationship and insuring that interpersonal relationships receive top priority within the practice.

This continuum of care is best illustrated in the groups' own cardiac catheterization laboratory. In this laboratory, outpatient procedures are performed away from the acute setting of the hospital, providing added convenience and comfort for the patient and the patient's family, as well as a more personal atmosphere. As a result, both patient and physician are better served.

Louisiana Cardiology Associates also operates one of the areas largest Coumadin Clinics. Coumadin is a drug frequently used as part of therapy in cardiovascular treatment and requires close monitoring. LCA provides this continuous monitoring, as well as patient education through their Coumadin Clinic. In addition, LCA has its own equipment for nuclear cardiology and its own echocardiogram machines with technicians specially trained to assist the cardiologist in these programs. As Louisiana Cardiology Associates looks to the future of cardiovascular treatment, emphasis will continue to be placed on the practice of early prevention. The group is affiliated with many wellness programs at various plants and businesses around town and is committed to helping area residents achieve and maintain optimal health. By maintaining its standard of excellence and compassion to the community, Louisiana Cardiology Associates continues to fill a critical need in the Baton Rouge community. ✣

The Red Stick located on the edge of the bluff of the Mississippi River on the campus of Southern University was sculpted by the internationally known artist Frank Hayden in 1976. The sculpture symbolizes the original site of the place called Baton Rouge (or to the once local Indians, "Red Stick").

Southern University

Overlooking the Mississippi River, and abundantly intertwined with Baton Rouge history and tradition, Southern University and A&M College is a comprehensive institution offering associate, baccalaureate, graduate, professional, and doctoral degree programs. The University is fully accredited by the Commission of Colleges of the Southern Association of Colleges and Schools*, and is part of the only historically black land grant university system in the United States. Southern University is also a member of the National Association of State Universities and Land Grant Colleges.

Chartered as Southern University in 1880 and first opened in New Orleans in 1881 with 12 students, the institution was relocated to Baton Rouge in 1914. After many years, the University expanded to other cities in the state creating Southern University at New Orleans in 1956, Southern University at Shreveport in 1964, and a cooperative extension livestock and horse facility in Baker. In addition, the Southern University Law Center, located in Baton Rouge, was established in 1947; and has graduated the majority of the state's African American lawyers.

In 1974, the state legislature organized the Southern University and A&M College System, comprised of the campuses in Baton Rouge, New Orleans, and Shreveport and the System's agricultural and cooperative extension programs. In that same year, the state legislature also established the Southern University Board of Supervisors, the System's management board. Dr. Leon R. Tarver II currently serves as the fourth president of the Southern University System, and Dr. Edward R. Jackson serves as chancellor of the Baton Rouge Campus.

Through the decades, Southern University has consistently met the educational needs of the community, while ascribing to the highest standards of academic leadership. Today, the Southern University System has a student population of nearly 16,000 students representing 41 states and 57 nations. The University has a long-standing commitment to providing educational access for students without regard to gender, ethnic background, religion, geographical or national origin, age, or physical challenges.

Understanding that learning must first be a journey of self-discovery and commitment, Southern University provides a core curriculum of liberal arts courses, quality academic programs, and support services to meet the needs and abilities of all students. The University is committed to providing a broad spectrum of programs and research activities and to vigilantly pursuing its mission of preparing students to compete globally in their respective professions and to engage in advanced studies in graduate and professional schools.

Southern University offers its students a unique educational sojourn that is rich in all aspects of the college experience from academics to athletics, community services to cooperative job training and more. The campus is located on Scott's Bluff overlooking the Mississippi River in North Baton Rouge. Legend holds that in 1699, the famous explorer Pierre Le Moyne, Sier d'lberville named the spot le Baton Rouge, French for "red stick", after he spotted a stick covered with fish heads and stained with the blood of animals where he came ashore. There is a monument erected on the spot that was sculpted by the noted artist, Frank Hayden to pay homage to the founding of Baton Rouge.

As Baton Rouge celebrates its 300th anniversary, the place that is Southern University and where Iberville first made his finding is still a place of discovery, of beauty and wonderment that captures the spirit and soul of the city's people. ✤

* 1866 Southern Lane, Decatur, Georgia 30033-4097; telephone 404-679-4501

The J.S. Clark Administration Building, located adjacent to the bluff of the Mississippi River is named after Dr. Joseph Samuel Clark, President 1913-1938. The J.S. Clark Administration Building houses the administrative offices of the Southern University System, the Board of Supervisors, and Southern University at Baton Rouge.

Marketplace

Mall of Louisiana

Photo by Brian Robbins Photography.

Since its grand opening in October 1997, the Mall of Louisiana has offered residents and visitors to Baton Rouge an opportunity to do something they have never done before: experience a mall "like no other."

Located just off I-10 at Bluebonnet Boulevard in Baton Rouge, the Mall of Louisiana offers an incredible array of more than 150 national and regional specialty stores. From top-draw anchor stores such as Dillard's, JC Penney, McRae's, Parisian, and Sears, to the more trendy shops like Banana Republic and Gap, the Mall of Louisiana has found a mix that not only draws shoppers from all parts of the region, but one that continues to welcome them back again and again.

As a super regional mall, encompassing 1.3 million square feet on two levels, the Mall of Louisiana has the tenant power to attract even the most discriminating shopper. Indeed, the complex's list of stores reads like a virtual "Who's Who" in the retail industry.

Stores such as Disney, Eddie Bauer, Express, and the Limited are finding they can expand their market share by taking advantage of the mall's excellent location in Southeast Baton Rouge, one of the city's fastest growing areas. The Mall of Louisiana's easy interstate access also makes it attractive to shoppers from as far as 70 miles away.

In addition, other stores, such as Ann Taylor, Abercrombie & Fitch, Aveda, Brookstone, Learningsmith, Restoration Hardware, and Williams-Sonoma have chosen to make their Capital City debut exclusively at the Mall of Louisiana.

But store strength and selection is not the only reason thousands of people flock to the Mall of Louisiana month after month. One look at this stunning complex reveals an architectural masterpiece featuring ceilings that soar, an abundance of natural light, and an elegant, welcoming entrance highlighted by a massive glassed-in cupola.

The Mall of Louisiana was designed with special family-oriented features including plush seating, family restrooms, abundant parking, and a state-of-the-art security camera system. Amenities also include a tempting food court where shoppers can enjoy ethnic as well as down-home cooking, and what any child would call the centerpiece of the Mall of Louisiana: an enchanting carousel.

While many shoppers would agree that simply going to the Mall of Louisiana is an event in itself, the complex, which was developed and is managed and leased by Jim Wilson & Associates, Inc., a prominent national real estate developer based in Montgomery, Alabama, also features special family-oriented events several times a year.

One of these events is the Mall of Louisiana's annual circus performance. Locals always look forward to this fall show where fearless circus

entertainers transform the complex's seven-story center court into a traditional Big Top, complete with high-wire acts, acrobatics, and other breathtaking performances.

When the weather turns colder, the Mall of Louisiana fills with excitement once again. This time dazzling lights set amid the traditional colors of the season showcase a winter wonderland for the arrival of Santa Claus. And at a time when anything seems possible, the Mall of Louisiana enhances the excitement with the addition of real snow.

Of course, in south Louisiana where snow is a rarity, the arrival of Santa Claus at the Mall of Louisiana is something children of all ages look forward to. Certainly, it's just one more reason why the Mall of Louisiana continues to be ..."A mall like no other." ✤

Hilton Baton Rouge

Since opening its doors to the capital city in 1976, the Hilton Baton Rouge has become a distinct landmark. Centrally located near Baton Rouge's bustling College Drive and Corporate Boulevard areas, the Hilton offers convenience to some of the city's prime destination points, including Louisiana State University and the State Capitol.

The hotel, which was the first flagship hotel to open in Baton Rouge, is also just a short drive from one of Louisiana's most celebrated and historical attractions, Nottoway Plantation, and is within an easy walking distance to some of the city's best shopping, theater, dining, and nightlife.

But location is not the only reason the Hilton Baton Rouge has become a popular choice among business and leisure travelers to the city. Indeed, in a state known for its good food, the Hilton Baton Rouge uses a simple recipe of southern hospitality, elegance, and its own world-class reputation to make it the city's favorite.

Just ask Hollywood. Some former guests to the hotel include Elvis Presley, Joan Rivers, Jackie Gleason, and most recently, George Clooney and Jennifer Lopez. Many politicians and dignitaries, including former presidents Ronald Reagan and George Bush, have also chosen to stay at the Hilton Baton Rouge when visiting the city.

Locals are also impressed with the Hilton Baton Rouge. With over 19,000 square feet of meeting space and 18 meeting and banquet rooms, it is the Hilton that many area business and organizational leaders call upon to host meetings, conventions, and other activities. The hotel is also a popular choice for social occasions, and has been included in the celebration of many local weddings.

With its reputation built solidly on service and attention to detail, it should come as no surprise that the Hilton Baton Rouge continually strives for perfection. For proof, visitors only need to take one step into the hotel's grand lobby. Here, a recent renovation plan has added a unique atmosphere and an inviting look to the hotel. Yes, there's still that same Southern charm the Hilton Baton Rouge has become known for, but now new designs and colors accentuate the state's natural heritage.

Colors such as evergreen woods and earthy fire tones captivate the visitor as well as an array of unique furniture finds and elegant antiques. The result: deep, rich colors that inspire a sense of warmth, recall the state's beautiful bayous and abundant wildlife, and remind guests that Louisiana is, truly, "Sportsman's Paradise."

Indeed, the hotel's renovation plan has not gone unnoticed. Once completed, the Hilton Hotels and Resorts bestowed its prestigious "Outstanding Renovation Award" to the Baton Rouge Hilton. The award cited renovations made not only to the hotel's lobby and bar, but also to its 300 oversized guest rooms, its expanded meeting and banquet facilities, and its restaurant, Cafe Acadian, where guests enjoy a mix of some of the area's popular Creole cuisines as well as regional fare.

Other accommodations and amenities at the Hilton Baton Rouge include a heated outdoor swimming pool, fitness center, and a complete business center offering fax, personal computer, and copying services. In addition, the Hilton Baton Rouge provides four private concierge level floors, and each guest room features several conveniences, including two phone lines with DATA ports for the business traveler.

The hotel, which stands 21 stories tall and graces the city's skyline, also offers some of the more spectacular views of Baton Rouge. Looking out from select rooms, guests can see all that is Baton Rouge, from its hustle and bustle of a growing capital city to its historical roots of LSU, state government, and the Mississippi River.

The Hilton Baton Rouge is operated by Davidson Hotel Company, a Memphis-based Hotel Management & Development Company which operates 26 hotels in 15 states. ✤

Radisson Hotel & Conference Center

With over 32,000 square feet of meeting space and a wide choice of meeting rooms, the Radisson Hotel & Conference Center Baton Rouge is the leader in accommodating the city's burgeoning need for premier meeting and convention facilities.

In fact, it was the city's strong economy and high demand for meeting space that prompted Executive Hotel Management (EHM) to buy the hotel in 1994.

EHM, which also owns two other upscale hotels in selected cities nationwide, immediately saw the economic impact new convention facilities would have on the city as well as on businesses throughout Baton Rouge. The Illinois-based firm went right to work, first affiliating the hotel with the worldwide Radisson Hotels, then beginning construction on new meeting and banquet facilities.

Interestingly, this new construction was designed around the hotel's rich history. The original facility was first built in 1974. When local investors decided to open it as a Sheraton Hotel, it quickly became *the* place to be in the city, and was frequented by politicians, local, national, and international celebrities.

But those happy days did not last long. When hard times hit the hotel industry in the late '80s, the hotel changed ownership numerous times.

Today, however, under the careful guidance of new management, the hotel is once again returning to its former days of splendor. From its graceful entryway to its elegant new lobby featuring fine oil paintings and richly detailed surroundings, guests are welcomed to Baton Rouge in a style that captures the unique blend of history, tradition, and culture of this fascinating city.

Indeed, the end result of renovations and refurbishing undertaken by EHM in the mid-'90s has been nothing short of exquisite. Revenues have risen each year since the opening of the Radisson. In addition, EHM has made a commitment to continuously update and improve the facility. By considering the hotel a long-term investment, EHM has ensured the Radisson will continue to be the area's first choice for state, regional, and national conventions.

Over the years, many groups and associations have selected the Radisson as the site for their convention including Alpha Kappa Alpha Sorority, American EX-P.O.W.'s, and Romantic Times, a convention of romance writers. In addition, the Radisson Hotel & Conference Center Baton Rouge has been credited with bringing business back to the Capital City.

"One group, the Gulf Coast Ammonia Producers, were looking to leave Baton Rouge. They had simply outgrown the city and could not find adequate facilities (for their convention). But we were able to accommodate them," said Kelly Hurtado, director of sales and marketing at the Radisson.

The Radisson offers flexible meeting and banquet space that includes the 15,000 square foot Premier Grand Ballroom, one of the largest ballrooms in the city of Baton Rouge. Whether it is a seminar, exhibit, training session, wedding reception, or awards banquet, the Radisson can easily accommodate groups from 5 to over 2,000 people.

Conveniently located at I-10 and College Drive near the downtown business district and Louisiana State University, the hotel offers comfortable, elegant surroundings, as well as a sincere, friendly, and professional staff dedicated to making each event at the Radisson a pleasurable one.

From planning the simplest meeting to the most elegant reception, the hotel's sales and catering teams follow a philosophy of service that ensures every event at the Radisson will not only be a success, but one that will be raved about for years to come.

The hotel also features several services in-house, such as a complete inventory of sound, lighting, and audio/visual equipment, helping to guarantee the ultimate success of each function.

Guests who stay at the Radisson enjoy luxurious accommodations. Whether it's a full-service restaurant and comfortable lounge or an outdoor swimming pool and state-of-the art health club, guests are sure to find the ideal way to relax and unwind.

The Radisson features 294 guest rooms, including 14 suites and a concierge level. Each room is expertly and handsomely decorated

with attention paid to even the smallest detail. In addition, guests have access to a wide array of amenities in each room including two telephones with data ports, a coffee maker, iron and ironing board, voice mail, computerized wake-up service, 24 hour room service, and Lodgenet entertainment systems. The private Plaza Club Level features the services of a concierge on duty, private checkin and out, breakfast, cocktails, hors d'oeuvres, turn down service, and private balconies.

Guests are treated exceptionally well. In fact, the hotel's strong focus on customer service has earned it the prestigious Radisson President's Award for four consecutive years. These awards are proof that at the Radisson Hotel & Convention Center Baton Rouge southern hospitality is not a cliche', it's simply how business is done.

Embassy Suites

Imagine waking up to the sounds of a relaxing waterfall, enjoying the beauty of a lush, green garden, or watching the showmanship of colorful fish as they swim all around you. Sound like you're in a dream?

Wait, it's not over.

Now add the intoxicating smell of just-brewed coffee and the sizzling sounds of your favorite breakfast foods being cooked to perfection.

Is it still a dream? No, at least not for the thousands of guests who have stayed at the Embassy Suites in Baton Rouge. Since opening in the Capital City in 1985, Embassy Suites has garnered a reputation as a virtual oasis for both corporate and leisure travelers.

The hotel provides 223 suites overlooking its grand centerpiece: a beautiful garden atrium featuring a waterfall and fishpond. The hotel, which is part of a network of Embassy Suites nationwide, is located just off the interstate, only minutes from downtown Baton Rouge, Louisiana State University, and other industries and attractions.

The hotel features a heated indoor pool, whirlpool, sauna, and exercise room. In addition, over 7,000 square feet of flexible meeting/banquet space is available to easily accommodate any event from a small meeting to a large wedding.

A $3.5 million renovation plan completed at the hotel, touched every aspect of the building's eight floors and added more amenities to every suite. The suites feature a two-room spacious living area complete with a refrigerator, wet bar, microwave, coffeemaker, and well-lit dining/work table. King or double beds are also available and every room features a dual-line telephone with data port, remote control TV, and a complimentary morning newspaper.

One favorite spot for guests at the Embassy Suites is, of course, the hotel's atrium. This "stress-free" zone offers a relaxing atmosphere and is the perfect spot for guests to unwind over casual conversation, read a book, or study. It is also an ideal place to enjoy cocktails during the Manager's Reception; a complimentary two-hour reception held each evening where guests are served beverages of their choice.

For guests wanting to experience a bit of the region's southern cooking, Embassy Suites features one of Baton Rouge's newest and most popular restaurants. The Memphis Bar-B-Q Co. is a national franchise renowned for its true smoked meats and other barbeque specialties. Of course, Louisiana's famous cuisine cannot go unnoticed, and the restaurant has capitalized on its locale. Look for several dishes featuring the area's famous blend of Cajun and Creole flavors.

Memphis Bar-B-Q Co., which also provides outside catering for almost any event, is operated by Premier Restaurant Operations. By selecting Memphis Bar-B-Q Co. as its hotel restaurant in late 1998, Embassy Suites in Baton Rouge became one of the first hotels in the area to begin outsourcing its restaurant.

"We're starting to see this more and more in this industry. Hotel companies are moving toward having a national company or franchise come in (to manage the restaurant). This allows the two entities to join together to promote the properties," said Don Zimmer, Director of Sales at the hotel.

But, according to Zimmer, that's not the only benefit, and Embassy Suites in Baton Rouge is taking full advantage of this industry change. "The addition of the Memphis Bar-B-Q Co. to the Embassy Suites here in Baton Rouge is wonderful," said Zimmer. "By allowing this upscale national franchise to do what they do best, which is to provide an excellent dining experience, then we are able to do what we do best."

And, according to Zimmer, that means providing a clean, comfortable atmosphere so that corporate and leisure travelers can have a pleasurable experience. Zimmer explained that the more than 95 employees at the hotel pride themselves on guest service. In fact, the hotel enforces a 100 percent satisfaction guarantee. If for any reason, the hotel fails to meet a guest's expectations, whether it concerns a meeting facility, room, or other service, the guest is not required to pay for that service. "I think that has made an impression on many people and accounts for our strong reputation," said Zimmer.

In order to provide this type of guest service, all Embassy employees receive extensive and ongoing training. In turn, the hotel strives to make those same employees feel just as special. Embassy Suites believes that by creating a pleasurable atmosphere for its employees, that same atmosphere and attitude will be transferred to guests.

Several celebrities and other noted visitors to the city have evidently agreed. Some of the more famous guest to stay at the Embassy Suites includes Oprah Winfrey, Aretha Franklin, Tanya Tucker, and the Temptations. Zimmer added that hotel employees enjoy the fans and the extra attention these celebrities bring to Embassy Suites.

Embassy Suites in Baton Rouge also offers wheelchair accommodations and senior citizen's discount. ✤

Mall at Cortana

It's been said that the best way to get to know a new city is to follow the locals. If that's true, then anyone wanting to know about shopping in Baton Rouge need only head straight to the Mall at Cortana.

Baton Rougeons call it the place to "power shop," and when you consider that the entire area encompassing the Mall at Cortana measures over two million square feet—then locals definitely know Cortana is the place to go.

Located in the physical center of the city, at Florida Boulevard and Airline Highway, Cortana provides convenient and easy access to and from every part of the greater Baton Rouge metropolitan area.

First opened in 1976, the mall was envisioned as the center of a shopping district called Cortana. Predicting that Baton Rouge would grow, a large tract of land was selected that remains available for expansion to meet future shopping needs of the community. A Wal-Mart store anchors that land.

In the mid-90s, as Baton Rouge began to grow and prosper, a wealth of new store construction began around the mall's perimeter, bringing power, selection, value, and diversity to Cortana. Today, stores such as Old Navy, Babies R Us, Gateway Country Store, Lowes Home Improvement Warehouse, and several restaurants serve the community's desire for one-stop convenience.

CortanaLand is a one of a kind play area fashioned to look like the Louisiana swamp. CortanaLand is lots of fun for the little ones and gives parents a chance to sit down and relax.

As a mainstay of the community, the Mall at Cortana is the heart of this shopping district. It is the largest mall in Louisiana and one of the largest malls in the South. The Mall at Cortana comprises 1.6 million square feet, and, at press time, features several large department stores in addition to offerings that include The Disney Store, Bath & Body Works, Eddie Bauer, The Limited, The Rolling Pin Kitchen Emporium, The Gap and its affiliated stores, Baby Gap and Gap Kids. The Mall at Cortana also features food and restaurants catering to all tastes and pocketbooks.

The Mall at Cortana remains one of the nation's top malls in sales per square foot and continues to lure shoppers with its premium selection, various amenities, and longtime reputation as a family destination.

The Mall at Cortana has always listened to its shoppers, adding services and those "little extras" that enhance the shopping experience. The physical structure has been well maintained, landscaped, and updated on an ongoing basis. A multi million-dollar series of renovations has been underway since 1987, modernizing the mall in phases so it can better serve its customers with style and beauty.

The Mall at Cortana is also a popular family destination. It offers a Kids Club, featuring special values and promotions just for children, and a Family Room where parents can tend to infants in private. For families with young children, there is the popular "CortanaLand," a $100 thousand play area built inside the mall so young children can run and play in a safe environment.

Special events are a hallmark at the Mall at Cortana. Several times a year, educational and fun activities are staged at the mall. Many of these events benefit charitable causes such as the United Way and the arts, among others.

Another service the mall provides is security. From parking lot escorts to a state-of-the-art surveillance system, the Mall at Cortana is a mall that cares about maintaining a comfortable environment for its shoppers.

As the city continues to grow and expand, the Mall at Cortana is also looking to extend its shopping district north of the mall, onto land already accessible as part of the master plan. And as shoppers in the 21st century continue to see more choices in selection and value offered at the Mall at Cortana, no doubt they will continue to "power shop" for fun, fashion, and excitement. Cortana offers the shopping experience which makes Baton Rougeons feel at home. ✤

Enterprise Index

Southern University
Southern Branch Post Office
Baton Rouge, Louisiana 70813
Phone: 225-771-4680
Fax: 225-771-5522
www.sus.edu
Page 147

Stupp Corporation
12555 Ronaldson Road
Baton Rouge, Louisiana 70807
Phone: 225-775-8800
Fax: 225-775-7610
E-mail: commercial@stupp.com
www.stuppcorp@stupp.com
Pages 100-101

Turner Industries
8687 United Plaza Boulevard,
Buliding IX
Baton Rouge, Louisiana 70809
Phone: 225-922-5050
1-800-288-6503
Fax: 225-922-5055
E-mail: webmaster@turner-industries.com
www.turner-industries.com
Pages 122-123

Uniroyal Chemical Company, Inc.
PO Box 397
Geismar, Louisiana 70734
Phone: 225-387-5112
225-673-8871
Fax: 225-673-0588
www.uniroyalchemical.com
Pages 94-95

Washer, Hill & Lipscomb
1744 Oakdale Drive
Baton Rouge, Louisiana 70810
Phone: 225-767-1530
Fax: 225-767-0018
Page 115

YMCA of Baton Rouge
350 South Foster
Baton Rouge, Louisiana 70806
Phone: 225-923-0653
Fax: 225-924-3609
Page 144

Bibliography

Bernard, Shane K. *Swamp Pop: Cajun and Creole Rhythm and Blues.* Jackson, Miss.: University Press of Mississippi, 1996.

Carleton, Mark T. *River Capital, An Illustrated History of Baton Rouge.* Tarzana, Calif.: American Historical Press, 1996.

Dalrymple, Margaret Fisher. *The Merchant of Manchac, The Letterbooks of John Fitzpatrick, 1768-1790.* Baton Rouge and London: Louisiana State University Press, 1978.

Din, Gilbert C. *The Canary Islanders of Louisiana.* Baton Rouge and London: Louisiana State University Press, 1998.

Dufour, Charles L. *Ten Flags in the Wind, the Story of Louisiana.* New York, Evanston, and London: Harper & Row, 1967.

East, Charles. *Baton Rouge, A Civil War Album.* Published by the author. Baton Rouge: 1977.

Favrot, J. St. Clair. *"Tales of Our Town, The First 100 Years".* Baton Rouge, Entree Magazine published by Louisiana National Bank.

Folse, John D. *The Evolution of Cajun and Creole Cuisine.* Gonzales, La.: Chef John Folse & Company Publishing, 1989.

Folse, John D. *Something Old and Something New.* Gonzales, La.: Chef John Folse & Company Publishing, 1989.

Fricker, Jonathan, et al. *Louisiana Architecture, A Handbook on Styles.* Lafayette: The Center for Louisiana Studies, University of Southwestern Louisiana, 1998.

Gould, Philip. *Cajun Music and Zydeco.* Baton Rouge and London: Louisiana State University Press, 1992.

Jones, Dennis, et al. *"The Kleinpeter Site: The History and Archaeology of a Multicomponent Site in East Baton Rouge Parish, Louisiana".* Louisiana Geological Survey, Anthropological Study No. 5, Baton Rouge, 1997.

Liebling, A.J. *The Earl of Louisiana.* Baton Rouge and London: Louisiana State University Press, 1960.

Meyers, Rosa. *A History of Baton Rouge, 1699-1812.* Baton Rouge: Louisiana State University Press, 19

Index

Printed in Mexico